Unpacking the 'Start-up City'

Maria Dodaro

Unpacking the 'Start-up City'

Entrepreneurship, Neoliberal Governance and Local Actors Agency

palgrave
macmillan

Maria Dodaro
Department of Philosophy, Sociology,
Education and Applied Psychology
University of Padua
Padova, Italy

ISBN 978-3-031-50211-8   ISBN 978-3-031-50212-5 (eBook)
https://doi.org/10.1007/978-3-031-50212-5

This Palgrave Macmillan imprint is published by the registered company Springer Nature Switzerland AG
The registered company address is: Gewerbestrasse 11, 6330 Cham, Switzerland

Paper in this product is recyclable.

Acknowledgements

My sincere thanks go firstly to each and every participant in this research, especially the young people who shared their stories and expectations for their entrepreneurial projects with me, often during the toughest phase. This work would have been impossible without them.

The book also owes a great deal to Lavinia Bifulco and Marisol García Cabeza who supported and encouraged me throughout this process, from my Ph.D. studies to the book's completion, giving me precious suggestions and constructive feedback on earlier drafts of this volume, which I hope I made appropriate use of. I would also like to thank Roberta Cucca and Ramon Ribera-Fumaz for the suggestions they made as external reviewers of the doctoral thesis this book was based on, and final doctoral committee members Enrica Morlicchio and Pedro Gallo De Puelles for their valuable insights and suggestions prior to the writing of this volume.

I am also grateful to Palgrave Macmillan/Springer Nature's editors for the opportunity to publish my research and to its support staff, especially Rachael Ballard and Saranya Siva. I am also very much indebted to the anonymous reviewers for their suggestions and constructive criticism, and to Isabelle Johnson for her patient and accurate English proofreading of the book.

A special thanks to my life companion Francesco for his careful reading of each chapter's drafts, for his precious suggestions, for encouraging me to keep going at the most challenging moments, and for the (great) lunches and dinners he made at its busiest periods. Thanks also go to my family for always being there, despite the geographical distance between us, and the great colleagues I met at the University of Milano-Bicocca, the University of Barcelona and the University of Padua for giving me much food for thought, and unforgettable moments of fun.

Contents

List of Figures

CHAPTER 1

Studying Entrepreneurship in European Cities

Abstract This chapter introduces some of the key theoretical, analytical and methodological foundations for the subsequent analysis of municipal entrepreneurship support policies (MESPs) in two southern European cities, Barcelona and Milan. It examines some of the long-term economic, social, political and cultural processes underlying the renewed social recognition and policy relevance accorded to entrepreneurship at different scales. This chapter also offers an overview of the general aims of the book: (a) to improve our understanding of convergence and divergence trends in urban policies and governance by combining the insights of neo-Marxian and neo-Weberian interpretative frameworks to the urban political economy and through cultural political economy and sociological analysis; (b) to contribute to filling a gap in the existing literature on the agency of local actors in neoliberal urban governance dynamics; and (c) to sheds light on the way local actors, including policy beneficiaries, reproduce, contest and resignify entrepreneurship policies and practices in highly individualised contexts.

Keywords Entrepreneurship policy · Agency · Neoliberal urban governance · Individualisation · Start-up city

M. Dodaro, *Unpacking the 'Start-up City'*,
https://doi.org/10.1007/978-3-031-50212-5_1

In 2009, *The Economist* published a special report on entrepreneurship entitled *Global Heroes* which argued that entrepreneurship had gone mainstream globally, with the support of policymakers of all ideological orientations, and a variety of actors including universities, financial investors and other pressure groups. As the title suggests, the report's emphasis is the figure of the "entrepreneur", a term used in this context in the Schumpeterian sense of an individual—who in the imaginary is typically white, male, creative, innovative and supremely talented and brilliant—capable of coming up with innovative solutions to as yet unsolved or unrecognised problems, including by combining profit and social goals. "Entrepreneurship has become cool", the report also pointed out. Entrepreneurship is presented not simply as a matter of economics, but as a mindset and key feature of contemporary society. In it we are seen as living in an "entrepreneurial society" which entails a specific type of individual characterised by entrepreneurial attitudes towards work and life in general, the reorientation and reorganisation of public action at various levels, and a new kind of social contract, namely a new balance between social rights and responsibilities.

I first read this report in 2013. I had just completed my university studies in economic and social sciences in one of the poorest regions of Italy and Europe (Calabria). Even in this peripheral area of Southern Italy, a pervasive discourse revolved around entrepreneurship as a panacea for all social ills exacerbated by the economic and financial crisis of 2008. The jobseekers problem, for example, but also a distressed local economy generating disinvestment and emigration, or the difficulties involved in finding new answers to growing social needs in a context of reduced public spending. The result has been an extensive and diverse body of policy initiatives implemented at all levels of government with a view to promoting entrepreneurship to foster active inclusion in the labour market and society, innovation and economic growth processes.

It is in this context that, fresh out of university, I was struck by entrepreneurship's potential as a viable alternative to emigration or a poor local labour market. I thus joined a young team working on an entrepreneurial project which received state funding set aside for socially innovative start-ups run by the under 35s. In this same period and context, after losing his job, my father set up his own business, a tyre fitting workshop, supported by a local business microcredit programme secured by regional funding for the unemployed over the age of 50. What struck me was that, despite their many differences, the two projects were relatively well-matched in an institutional agenda focusing on enhancing entrepreneurship in its disparate forms. This personal experience reinforced my interest in entrepreneurship studies, its significance and the ambivalence that ultimately underlies entrepreneurial practices and policies. It is an interest that has been further nurtured by the growing relevance of entrepreneurship as an activation policy tool for both employment and economic development. Since then, support for entrepreneurship, and start-ups in particular, has come to play a central role in development policies both regionally and in large cities around the world. In these cities public and private actors have supported the development of public action in this area, under the "start-up city" label, leveraging the most striking and positive image of entrepreneurship. The large cities have taken on special and growing symbolic and material relevance to contemporary entrepreneurship and related support policies fuelling the start-up rhetoric as a culturally hegemonic ideal and model (Fiorentino, 2018). In fact, cities embody an enabling ground for technology transfer and the creation of new businesses, including high-growth and high-tech start-ups which are experiencing a process of concentration in a shrinking number of large cities (Burroni & Trigilia, 2011; European Commission, 2016; Houston & Reuschke, 2017; Mind the Bridge, 2018).

The significance of the phenomenon has prompted a new specific strand of literature, especially on the role of entrepreneurship as part of neoliberalising trends in urban policies and governance, with an emphasis on the making of new (neoliberal) subjectivities (Fiorentino, 2018; Levenda & Tretter, 2020; McNeill, 2017; Moisio & Rossi, 2020; Simpson, 2021). Rossi and Di Bella (2017) have noted changes underway in this respect which they define with the term "start-up urbanism", that is, a model of governance designed to reshape cities primarily in accordance with the needs of entrepreneurs and entrepreneurship ethos. Drawing on Foucault, and philosophers such as Hardt and Negri, Agamben, Virno and Debord, this model of governance is portrayed as conveying a political and cultural message aimed at creating the conditions for a self-governing entrepreneurial society that values and seeks entrepreneurial subjectivity (Rossi, 2017; Rossi & Di Bella, 2017). Start-up urbanism, therefore, constitutes an updated and more pervasive version of the "urban entrepreneurialism" theorised by David Harvey more than thirty years ago, since "today's post-recession societies are witnessing an expansion in the process of entrepreneurialisation, involving society as a whole and the self" (ivi, p. 1010).

However, there is a great deal of scholarly disagreement over the impact of neoliberal capitalism on cities (Enright et al., 2018; Le Galès, 2016; Pinson & Morel Journel, 2017). Several scholars claim that neoliberal ideas are neither simply imposed nor merely resisted locally but rather form part of a repertoire of local action implemented in specific socio-economic contexts by manifold actors who hybridise diverse logics and ideas, combine a range of resources and pursue divergent objectives, meaning that their actions sometimes result in ambivalent and unexpected outcomes. From this perspective, structural constraints interlock with the agency grounded within social actors' governance spaces and everyday practices (policymakers, stakeholders, practitioners, individuals and groups), resulting in processes which depend on multilevel formal and informal social, economic, cultural and political relations (Kazepov et al., 2022; Le Galès, 2016; Pinson & Morel Journel, 2017; Pradel et al., 2020).

This book draws from neo-Marxian and neo-Weberian scholarly traditions to the urban political economy and dialogues with empirical observations made during my doctoral studies in 2017–2018 in the European cities of Milan and Barcelona to examine what lies behind the "start-up city" label. To this end, I will take stock of the variety of entrepreneurship support programmes implemented in both cities. Referring to entrepreneurship support programmes, in its broadest sense, averted the risk of excluding cases which are potentially difficult to analyse through the more limited category of start-ups, but are nevertheless attributable to this discursive field. In so doing, the book examines municipal entrepreneurship support policies (hereafter also MESPs) and addresses the lack of in-depth empirical knowledge of this topic. From a European perspective, the book seeks to fill the gap identified in the literature on start-up urbanism on the agency of social actors, and the agency/action interplay with the ideal models of individual subjectivity and urban governance this evokes. The overall aim is to improve our understanding of convergence trends as well as agency in a way that encompasses the influence of the local social, economic and political-cultural context, while also examining the representations, motivations, intentions and room for manoeuvre of local actors involved in the field, including policy beneficiaries.

An overarching argument throughout this book is that theoretical and empirical insights point in the direction of understanding convergence trends towards neoliberal modes of governance and the enactment of agency as relational, differentiated and rooted in local contexts—understood as places where multi-scalar spatial, economic, social and institutional processes interact. It does so by presenting novel knowledge on urban entrepreneurship support policies in the landscape of economic, social and cultural changes arising from several interdependent trajectories, including territorial reorganisation of the economy and public powers, technological innovation, financialisation, changing welfare systems and trends towards greater individualisation of risks and responsibilities currently reshaping the socio-institutional framework in which entrepreneurship practices and policies takes shape.

1.1 Entrepreneurship in Contemporary Cities

The rise of the start-up phenomenon in the political agenda and public discourse has, particularly since the 2008 crisis, been trumpeted as the best way to revitalise economies, foster knowledge-based societies and promote innovation, economic development and social inclusion "from below", i.e. through processes driven by individuals, small firms and local governments (Eurocities, 2013; Fiorentino, 2018; Pollio, 2020; Rossi & Di Bella, 2017). This rise has taken shape within the tangle of long-term economic, social, political and cultural processes underlying the renewed social recognition and policy relevance accorded to entrepreneurship. The starting point is the role cities play in the globalisation and reorganisation processes underway in capitalism, with a focus on their effects on urban policies and governance. Growth and competitiveness imperatives will be discussed with a view to highlighting the way in which cities have been materially and discursively constructed as privileged sites for economic growth and technological and market innovation, and the part they play in the development of models of entrepreneurial subjectivity in the more general context of individualisation processes. What follows will illustrate some of the main processes underlying local public action for entrepreneurship support, for introductory purposes only and with no attempt at a thoroughgoing overview of the plurality of aspects involved.

European Cities in a Globalised World. The relevance of entrepreneurship and its local dimension is set against the backdrop of the rescaling/

re-territorialisation dynamics within both economic and political-institutional spaces which globalisation has triggered. A number of scholars have highlighted the growing importance of cities (rescaling) in global economies following on from the rise of the service economy (Sassen, 2006) and the hollowing out of the state (Bagnasco & Le Galès, 2000; Brenner, 2004; Le Galès, 2002). For Rhodes (2007), for example, nation states have been hollowed out by pressures exerted at various levels: from above, due to their growing international interdependence; from below, because of the increasing role played by local networks of multiple actors and marketisation processes; and sideways, influenced by private sector agencies, parastatal bodies and epistemic communities (p. 1248). Although the hollowing out of the state thesis is a matter of debate, a number of authors with a range of perspectives have agreed that cities are central to the reorganisation of capitalist production and reproduction processes (especially the neo-Marxist school of thought) and political powers (especially the neo-Weberian political economy tradition). Harvey (1989) argued that the state empties out when it loses the power to control international capital flows and act as a bargaining centre, with these functions shifting to the local level, leading to a reorientation of urban policy and governance in the direction of a model he described as "entrepreneurial", aimed at bolstering regions' growth, attractiveness and competitiveness. Harvey's work paved the way for an influential scholarly current on urban neoliberalisation. As Peck (2014, p. 399) put it, "if in the 1980s municipal administrations were beginning to 'behave' in an entrepreneurial manner, since then the late neoliberal city has ingested and internalised the entrepreneurial logics itself". In general, reference is made to urban policies and governance as neoliberal with a view to highlighting the growing relevance of market-oriented approaches, the tendency to prioritise growth and competitiveness over redistributive and social justice goals and to promote responsible and entrepreneurial subjectivity (Sternberg, 2023).

However, critical views on the neoliberal city thesis have emerged (Le Galès, 2016; Pinson & Morel Journel, 2017). Neo-Weberian urban scholars, for example, have highlighted the distinctive characteristics of the European city (Kazepov et al., 2021). From this standpoint, the urban entrepreneurialism framework is capable of explaining only certain aspects of the change dynamics at work in European cities. Its relevance is acknowledged but in a way that is limited and conditioned by interest group fragmentation, the role played by public institutions, social movements and civil society, and the continuing significance of national and local welfare systems. The small to medium size of European cities, and social structures based on the resilience of the middle and lower-middle classes, have been identified as equally important features of a "European city model", marked by a tendency towards a balance between growth and social cohesion (Bagnasco & Le Galès, 2000; Kazepov et al., 2021; Le Galès, 2016, 2018; Pradel & García, 2021).

However, several critical scholars have acknowledged the limitations inherent in adopting a totalising, coherent and systematic view of urban neoliberalisation processes. Brenner et al. (2010), in particular, have shed light on the diverse trajectories of urban change under neoliberalism, understood as a "variegated" process that is "*simultaneously* patterned, interconnected, locally specific, contested and unstable" (p. 184). Davies and Blanco (2017) emphasised the role of urban politics in containing neoliberalism and the role that the "multiple logics" of the local (e.g. interests, values, objectives, institutional legacies) play in opening up the "different forms of situated agency" that undermine the coherence of neoliberal governance models (p. 1518). Sternberg (2023) highlighted how these are mediated by specific socio-political institutions and cultures and mobilise diverse rhetoric, meanings, representations and measures, depending on context.

European cities have certainly retained their specific antidotes against the effects of neoliberalisation. However, there is evidence that recent socio-economic and institutional transformations have undermined the ability of European cities to counterbalance the imperatives of growth and competition with redistributive goals (Cucca & Ranci, 2017; Le Galès, 2018; Ranci et al., 2014). The pressures on the European city model partly stem from the forms of retrenchment implicit and explicit to welfare states (Bifulco, 2017; Castel, 2004; Mingione, 2018; Streeck, 2014) on which it largely depends (Kazepov et al., 2021). Furthermore, the pervasiveness of competitiveness as a key reference for urban policies in contexts of economic restructuring influenced by processes of de-industrialisation, financialisation, tertiarisation of the economy, flexibilisation of labour markets and impoverishment also play a role. As Pradel and García stressed: "European policies and policy approaches have counteracted - a great deal more than in other parts of the world - the consequences of urban restructuring under the influence of generalised neoliberal thinking. However, the competitive city drift has affected the policy priorities of city leaders" (2021, p. 546). In this respect, the changing geography of capitalism along with the dissemination of the "new regionalist paradigm" of economic growth—also promoted by European regional policy—have contributed to constructing cities and regions as key competitiveness and economic growth hubs (Keating, 2017), both discursively and materially. Cities and regions have been conceptualised in this context as "neo-Marshallian nodes in global networks" (Amin & Thrift, 1992), "integrated unit[s] of production" (Sabel, 1994), "local production systems" (Crouch et al., 2004) or "innovative milieu" leveraging common values, knowledge, trust and economic specialisation (Camagni, 2002). This has all helped legitimise and feed the construction of "economic imaginaries" (Jessop, 2004; Sect. 1.2) such as the "start-up city" or city as an "entrepreneurial ecosystem", naming (and thought) processes regarding cities that are performative in nature, assigning central importance to certain policies, actions and actors over others and orienting the goals, aspirations and interests of various urban actors (Borelli, 2012).

Cities as Entrepreneurial Ecosystems. The economic and statehood rescaling processes underway are the background from which the "entrepreneurial ecosystem" concept emerged. It refers to the "place-based social and cultural conditions for creating the robust environments, the ecosystems, in which entrepreneurship can thrive" (Levenda & Tretter, 2020, p. 491). Within the current scientific and public debate, these ecosystems often overlap with cities which are increasingly conducive to business-friendly environment creation and capable of attracting entrepreneurs and supporting innovative entrepreneurship (European Commission, 2016). The recent rise of the start-up city fits into this scenario. It developed both as a city branding strategy, and as a concrete set of services, infrastructure, public–private partnerships and incentives contributing to connoting the start-up economy (digital, high-tech, high-growth) as predominantly city-based (Fiorentino, 2018; Pollio, 2020; Rossi & Di Bella, 2017).

The literature on start-up urbanism (Rossi & Di Bella, 2017) has stressed the part played by start-ups in shaping urban governance and economies. Notably, scholars in this field have noted the performative role of start-up rhetoric, and its ranking and think tank apparatus (McNeill, 2017), in spreading the same kind of action supporting entrepreneurship in cities around the world (Fiorentino, 2018). Start-up city and entrepreneurship policies are interpreted from this perspective as devices—in the Foucauldian sense of a set of discourses, institutions, norms, architectural structures, scientific statements, ideas, values and principles—designed to govern society. This resonates with critical entrepreneurship studies which discussed the ideological implications of the "hegemonic positive discourse" of entrepreneurship (Essers et al., 2017, p. 5), i.e. a vague, prescriptive, decontextualised and depoliticised narrative. The latter is seen, on the one hand, as fostering competition, market rationality, economic calculus and autonomy as universal regulatory and moral standards and, on the other, as obscuring the multiple ways entrepreneurship is conceived and implemented in favour of a Schumpeterian conception of the phenomenon.

Entrepreneurship. The revival of Schumpeter's thesis in both economic and managerial studies and general public discourse contributed to articulating an imaginary in which entrepreneurs are seen as *the* innovators par excellence, with an ability to provide "creative" rather than "adaptive responses" to socio-economic changes and problems via action "outside of the range of existing practice" (Schumpeter, 1947, p. 150). Critical entrepreneurship studies consider this view limited, primarily due to its tendency to constrain entrepreneurship "within the dictum of profit maximisation and wealth creation" (Essers et al., 2017, p. 2) and its inclination to overlook alternative meanings and practices (such as collective and value-based entrepreneurship practices). From this perspective, this view is also deemed to contribute to the prevalence of rational-functionalist approaches in researching this phenomenon. Criticisms of such approaches revolve around focusing theoretical reflection and empirical research on the determinants of entrepreneurship, assuming a positive character and almost exclusively stressing its more "genuine" forms, which can be classified as "opportunity-based entrepreneurship". This is the category used in the academic literature to identify entrepreneurship originating in the identification of market opportunities, as opposed to that arising out of necessity and, in particular, from the absence of labour market alternatives (necessity-driven entrepreneurship) (GEM, 2018; Sheehan & Namara, 2015).

Overall, entrepreneurship is a multifaceted phenomenon and "few concepts reflect more scope and ambiguity" (Reynolds & Curtin, 2007, p. 2). In most cases, academics and decision-makers rely on a broad understanding of entrepreneurship as a process involving setting up new business/professional organisations. This is also the case with the Global Entrepreneurship Monitor (GEM), a networked consortium of national teams conducting global entrepreneurship surveys, primarily affiliated with academic institutions. In these surveys, individual entrepreneurs are defined as "every person engaged in any behaviour related to new business creation, no matter how modest" (Reynolds et al., 2005, p. 209). The notion of entrepreneurship is also often used interchangeably with that of self-employment, with autonomy being seen as the main distinguishing feature from employed status. However, entrepreneurship's multifaceted character tends to be poorly appreciated in both the literature and the public discourse, in favour of an essentially dualistic interpretation of the phenomenon juxtaposing the "bright" side of opportunity-based entrepreneurship with the "dark" side of necessity-driven entrepreneurship, characterised, for example, by poor profit margins, insufficient social safety nets and longer working hours than employees (Sheehan & Namara, 2015). It is a dark side which potentially also hides low employment security and low pay (Ahl & Marlow, 2021; Caraher & Reuter, 2017), a situation unlikely to fit with the image of entrepreneurship as an always positive (and depoliticised) phenomenon, papering over its contradictions, values, ideas and conceptualisation of problems and solutions (Essers et al., 2017; Perren & Jennings, 2005). The growing importance of policies supporting entrepreneurship requires shining the spotlight on both the socio-cultural, value and normative framework which underlies the abstract and elusive concept of entrepreneurship, and the ways in which different social actors reproduce, contest and resignify the entrepreneurial "device". As with other neoliberal depictions of urban change, there is thus a need to supplement the picture with analyses that are, on the one hand, context-sensitive and capable of providing a more in-depth account of actors' points of view and room for agency (Pinson, 2022; Pinson & Morel Journel, 2017) and, on the other, capable of taking the overarching context of public action at the local level into account including, in this specific case, forms of social organisation and particularly topical forms of individualisation.

Individualisation. Several scholars have contended that entrepreneurship and the entrepreneur fully embody the model of socialisation demanded by the individualisation trends which permeate contemporary society (Peters, 2001; Serrano Pascual & Martín Martín, 2017). The individualisation concept in fact provides an interesting lens through which to interpret the ambivalence of entrepreneurial practices and policies and, in particular, the way in which neoliberal trends may interlock in this field with a growing demand for subjectivity, autonomy and self-realisation spaces that—this is one of the book's main arguments—contribute to shape entrepreneurship policies at the city level.

In sociology, the concept of individualisation is generally employed in reference to changes in the individual-society relationship and the ways in which societies and individuals are undergoing processes that emphasise individual autonomy, personal choice, flexible adaptation, self-expression, and the decline of traditional social structures. Overall, individualisation refers to the historical and social process of de-traditionalisation, that is the breaking down of binding, sometimes oppressive, social bonds and the building of modernity as a society of individuals free to self-determine and construct their identities beyond social roles defined within traditional institutions (such as family, local community) (Mingione, 2018; Paci, 2005). The way this has been taking shape within the context of the crisis of modernity (Harvey, 1993) and the growth of uncertainty and social insecurity (Castel, 2004, 2016) in the most recent capitalist transformations is one of the main focuses of sociological reflection. The latter has, in particular, highlighted the contradictions arising from a growing requirement to, and at the same time demand for, autonomy and freedom of self-realisation, on the one hand, and the increasing constraints acting on self-determination, on the other (Beck & Beck-Gernsheim, 2002). Individuals disembedded from collective identities and organisations are, in fact, compelled to view themselves as responsible for their own living conditions, assess options and make their life decisions on the basis of increasingly de-standardised and non-linear life trajectories, all set against the backdrop of the retrenchment of the postwar welfare state. Welfare state crises have contributed to shifting the responsibility for social protection and well-being increasingly to the individual (Castel, 2004) and making individualisation "the most advanced form of socialization dependent on the market" (Beck, 1992, p. 131), turning it from a "a project of qualitative self-emancipation" to a "systemic prerequisite of individual performance" (Borghi, 2011, p. 325). From this perspective, individualisation has become a process with which to maximise and improve personal performance rather than an emancipation project, from education to employment, a matter of proving one's adaptability and ability to strategise risks and opportunities, and navigate a less predictable social landscape. The result is lives turned into projects to be developed reflexively while systemic contradictions become individual events frequently perceived in terms of personal fault or failure to be actively addressed regardless of structural conditioning and inequalities (Beck, 1992).

However, while individualisation processes cannot disregard structural forms of social conditioning, the importance of active and reflexive dispositions should not be neglected either. For example, sociological findings on young people—the focus of Chapters 4 and 5 of this volume—suggest that reflexive dispositions increasingly matter but that they are, at the same time, unevenly structured (Nico & Caetano, 2021; Spanò, 2019; Walther, 2005; Woodman & Vanderharst, 2021) and dependent on the social and institutional context in which young people's lives are embedded.

Agency. While structural factors and context help delineate the framework of constraints and opportunities in which individual actions and aspirations take shape, individuals are also bearers of the ideas, values, needs, resources and strategies that help both inform policies and shape social, economic, political and cultural specificities, and not mere endpoints in processes taking place above their heads. Concepts such as "bounded agency" or "situated agency" (Evans, 2002) have been formulated to account for the constraints of the economic, social and political-cultural contexts influencing individual beliefs, aspirations and actions, on the one hand, and the room for agency on the other (see also Nico & Caetano, 2021). The definition of agency remains controversial. As Threadgold et al. have pointed out (2021) agency is often a matter of forms of resistance to structural forces, i.e. existing social, economic and political conditions. For example, in their study on the agential capabilities of young people working in the hospitality industry in Australia, they argued that "structure is what happens when existing inequalities are reproduced, and agency is what happens when they are changed for the good. If they are changed for the worse, even through the active efforts of young people, then that is structure as well, because these actions are seen to be structurally determined and therefore not agentic. This is what we called the 'black box' of agency" (p. 18).

For clarity on the concept of agency, Katz (2004) elaborated three categories of particular use in accounting for "the different strategies that people use to stay afloat and even reformulate the conditions and possibilities of their everyday lives". These are resilience, reworking and resistance. Resilience concerns "small acts" and "ways to get by each day" (p. 244). It consists of ways of coping with everyday circumstances without necessarily altering existing power relations and social structures. As far as reworking practices are concerned these "are those that alter the conditions of people's existence to enable more workable lives and create more viable terrains of practice". Reworking practices "tend to be driven by explicit recognition of problematic conditions and offer focused, often pragmatic, responses to them". With such practices people's "interests are not so much in challenging hegemonic power as in attempting to undermine its inequities on the very grounds on which they are cast" (p. 247). Lastly, resistance involves consciousness-building and has an explicitly oppositional character. More to the point, it includes practices which "draw on and produce a critical consciousness to confront and redress historically and geographically specific conditions of oppression and exploitation at various scales" (p. 251). As can be inferred, the differences between the three forms of agency also consist of diverse awareness of social conditioning. In using this distinction and to avert the risk Threadgold et al. (2021) stressed, this book will focus on social actors' perspectives, including young beneficiaries of entrepreneurship support measures in Barcelona and Milan, and take opinions and the meanings they associate with entrepreneurship practices and policies seriously.

Individualisation and Public Action. Public action (see Sect. 1.2) and, more specifically, policies are relevant to the individualisation process context as they can contribute to widening or narrowing the spaces for agency, depending on whether they adopt it as a prerequisite (Borghi, 2011) or use it as a promotion and development sphere (Bifulco, 2012). The rise of activation as the main policy paradigm in social policy has led, over time, to agency being largely regarded as a prerequisite. Individualisation processes themselves take the form of a "regime of justification" (Boltanski & Thévenot, 2006). As Borghi noted: "individualization is invoked as one of the most relevant historical pressures underlying the 'activation turn' in social and labour market services and welfare policies in general" (2011, p. 326). Although there is no single agreed definition of the concept, there is consensus among scholars that activation consists of a policy paradigm according to which, firstly, social inclusion must occur through participation in the market (primarily the labour market), and secondly, welfare states should pursue this as their main goal (van Berkel & Møller, 2002), an ethos which is fully embodied and taken to its extreme by entrepreneurship (Lodigiani & Scippa, 2014). As Chapter 3 will discuss in greater depth, entrepreneurship and self-employment are now key instruments in the European Employment Strategy (EES) framework and aim to activate jobseekers through alternatives to employment as well. The promotion of "inclusive entrepreneurship policies" has been encouraged "to ensure that all people have an opportunity to be successful as an entrepreneur" and that more people can be moved "into work via self-employment to allow people an opportunity to participate economically and socially, and to generate income for themselves" (OECD/European Union, 2017, p. 15). Its target groups are those least represented among entrepreneurs and/or most struggling to enter the labour market. These include women, migrants, people with disabilities, the older unemployed (OECD/European Commission, 2017) and, especially, young people, a key target in activation programmes in general (Bifulco & Mozzana, 2016; Crespo & Serrano, 2004; Walther, 2005). Young people are, in fact, increasingly called on to play an active role in building their own identities and lives (Spanò, 2017).

Policies, in this context, are designed to foster the development of "free, autonomous, self-regulating individuals" and "the responsibilisation of individuals as moral agents" guided by leitmotivs such as "excellence", "performance" and "enterprise" (Peters, 2001, pp. 66–68). This is the model of subjectivity incentivised by "enterprise culture" policies. Having emerged in the UK under Margaret Thatcher, enterprise culture is now a central motif in the neoliberal political ideology, emphasising the values of market rationality, economic calculation and individual responsibility as universal normative and moral standards (Bröckling, 2016; Peters, 2001).

Studying Urban Entrepreneurship Policies. In the light of the above, support for entrepreneurship in cities takes shape at the intersection between three levels. The first of these is the macro-level of the socio-economic and political-cultural dynamics informing both public and individual action. This is linked to territorial reorganisation processes in the economy and public powers in the context of globalisation, the dissemination of neoliberal regulation models, individualisation processes, changes affecting labour markets and welfare systems, and the way in which these dynamics intertwine with changes in urban governance. The second is the meso-level covering the specificities of national and local contexts, and the third, the individual and subjective levels. The interaction between these levels influences the ways entrepreneurship is conceived in a given historical context and time and, as we will see, results in locally embedded macro-process redefinition.

Of note in this respect is the importance that cultural and positional factors have historically been accorded in entrepreneurship, as sociology has stressed since its advent. For instance, Sombart highlighted that entrepreneurship can be viewed as a viable alternative path to economic success for marginal social classes or groups or those whose social status is diminishing. Weber highlighted the role of beliefs, ethics and culture in the self-initiative characteristic of entrepreneurs (Gallino, 1978). Recent research in Italy on the institutional drivers of local economic development has underlined the local embeddedness of entrepreneurship (Bagnasco, 1977; Becattini, 2002) finding, for example, that obstacles to upward social mobility are some of the main self-employment drivers in Italy (with some of the highest rates in Europe). The reasons people leave the labour market to embark on self-employment or entrepreneurial paths were primarily to be found in the specific characteristics of Italian production. Mostly, fragmentation and the prevalence of defensive competition strategies by firms, i.e. focused on reducing labour costs, with their negative repercussions on opportunities for upward social mobility (Barbieri & Bison, 2004; Panichella, 2013). Sociological theories complicate the essentially dualistic interpretation most in vogue in entrepreneurship studies since, for instance, a structural lack of career opportunities in the labour market is a key driver which cannot easily be associated with pure opportunity nor necessity-based motivations. This suggests a need to look at entrepreneurship also as part of individual strategies sensitive to local specificities and a complex phenomenon in which multiple factors are at play at different levels.

In conclusion to this section, we have seen that the revival of entrepreneurship in the public and political domains has found fertile terrain in the context of the rise of neoliberalism and individualisation processes. Within this framework, several scholars see the city being configured as the preferred context for the entrepreneurialisation of society and the making of entrepreneurial subjectivity. This book inquiries into empirical evidence collected in Milan and Barcelona to understand whether and how policies supporting entrepreneurship entail a radicalisation of neoliberalism in these European cities, that is if, and to what extent, they reproduce/radicalise models of governance and intervention anchored to a conception of the city mostly as a business-friendly environment focusing on urban competitiveness and individual activation and responsibilisation as the main levers for social and labour inclusion. Furthermore, the book explores the extent to which policies supporting entrepreneurship adhere to a Schumpeterian ethos and whether there is room for other organisational forms in them and if so how much. A further aim is to gain insights into the distributional and social inequality implications of this, examining the relationship between entrepreneurship support, on the one hand, and individualisation and responsibilisation processes, on the other.

In so doing, the book examines the ability of local policy actors, including beneficiaries, to hybridise multiple logics, pool a range of resources and enact strategies capable of orienting entrepreneurship support policies in the direction of divergent and unpredictable outcomes. By investigating the way local actors reproduce, interpret but also challenge trends towards greater individualisation, inequalities and neoliberalisation in Barcelona and Milan, this book argues for a multi-scalar and nuanced understanding of municipal entrepreneurship support policies, as well as of urban neoliberalisation.

1.2 Insights from Cultural Political Economy and the Sociology of Public Action

The book draws on political economy and sociology to examine the way in which various factors taking shape at different scales interact in the rise and consolidation of urban policies designed to foster entrepreneurship. Notably, the book owes much to the analytical and heuristic approaches of cultural political economy (CPE) and the sociology of public action.

CPE is a current of thought developed in the early 2000s by a group of scholars at Lancaster University (Jessop, 2010; Jessop & Sum, 2010; Sum, 2009) who emphasised the relevance of the cultural dimension in political economy. From CPE the book embraces, first of all, its recognition of the relevance of ideas and representations in policymaking and, more specifically, the role played by "economic imaginaries". Economic imaginaries are described as "semiotic systems[1] that frame individual subjects'

[1] CPE assumes that social phenomena are compounded by a semiotic and an extrasemiotic dimension. The semiotic dimension relates to culture, representations, the "intersubjective production of meaning" (Jessop, 2010, p. 337). Extra-semiotic refers to

lived experience" and "give meaning and shape to the 'economic' field" (Jessop, 2010, p. 344). Examples explored from this perspective are "competitiveness" (Sum, 2009), the knowledge-based economy (Jessop, 2004) and the "start-up society" (Simpson, 2021). These are imaginaries which have been selected, retained and institutionalised over time and exert performative functions, i.e. they contribute to orienting and signifying public and individual actions.

From both CPE and the sociology of public action perspectives (Lascoumes & Le Galès, 2012), interpreting policies requires analysing the policy paradigms within which they take shape and reproduce, with paradigm defined as a "framework of ideas and standards that specifies not only the goals of policy and the kind of instruments that can be used to attain them, but also the very nature of the problems they are meant to be addressing" (Hall, 1993, p. 279). In line with the Bourdesian meaning of the term, each "field" of public action can be seen, from this perspective, as a sort of microcosm of individual and group relationships and conflicts in which what is at stake is the positions it is possible to hold within it and the resources and power to define rules, values and norms by leveraging a variable mix of economic (i.e. wealth), cultural (education, expertise, knowledge) and social (relationships, social networks) capital. Referring to public action rather than public policy enables a shift of focus to this aspect of relationship, coordination and conflict between different actors (not only the state) and the multiplicity of aspects underlying decision-making processes, starting with agenda-setting, in which theories, ideas and values contribute to the definition of problems to be addressed and viable options (Bifulco, 2017).

In greater detail, Lascoumes and Le Galès (2012) developed an analytical scheme ("the pentagon of public action") that identified five essential dimensions of public action: actors, institutions, representations, processes and outcomes. Action can be performed by a multiplicity of actors, both individual and collective, and involve state actors (local authorities, nation states, international public institutions), private actors, civil society organisations and individuals. These are guided by material and symbolic interests and resources to varying degrees and refer to diverse timeframes—i.e. they may have differing short- and/or long-term goals.

the material and structural dimension, i.e. "the materiality of social relations and the constraints involved in processes that also operate 'behind the backs' of the relevant agents" (Jessop & Sum, 2001, p. 94).

Moreover, they are interdependent, and this interdependence takes shape at various scales. Their action is influenced by this interdependence, alongside the other dimensions which make up the pentagon. At the same time, they have some autonomy in formulating strategies and taking decisions (agency) that can steer public action towards multiple ends. Representations are the cognitive and normative frameworks that give meaning to actions. In particular, they are part of the process by which social and political issues are constructed, i.e. the dynamics by which we define which issues are relevant—and which are not—and whether and how they can be addressed, linking this process to values and symbols. Institutions comprise norms, rules, routines and procedures which guide interactions between actors. Processes are the result of dynamic interaction between the three dimensions, i.e. different actors, with their interests and resources, embedded in cognitive and normative frames, phases and scales. They focus on how actors mobilise, build alliances, coalitions and conflicts within this framework and reflect power relations. In this regard, Bifulco (2017) observed that "there is broad agreement amongst researchers on the fact that policymaking does not coincide with rational decision-making and formal rules but is interwoven with negotiation, dynamics of framing and reframing, conflict and agreement building, so that adaptations and changes are all part of it, in the same way as incoherence and unpredictability" (p. 1). In this sense, public action is shaped not only by multiple actors, pre-existing representations and the institutions that "construct" social reality, but also by negotiations, conflicts and adaptation mechanisms which may generate incoherence, shifts, changes and unpredictable outcomes.

The CPE and sociology of public action approaches supply an alternative to the functionalism that tends to characterise studies on entrepreneurship practices and policies, by allowing their socio-political and cultural dimensions to be taken account of, as well as the interplay between economic, social, political and socio-institutional[2] processes. The sociology of public action also provides the means with which to examine the shift from government to governance (Bifulco, 2017; Lascoumes & Le Galès, 2012; Moini, 2013). Just as with other policy fields, urban policies supporting entrepreneurship are also influenced, as the following

[2] The term "institution" is used in the sociological sense to indicate "regulative, normative, and cultural-cognitive elements that, together with associated activities and resources, provide stability and meaning to social life" (Scott, 2014, p. 56).

chapters will show, by actors and institutions operating at both vertical (supranational, e.g. the EU) and horizontal (local)[3] levels of governance, and by the interaction between these different actors at multiple scales. Finally, focusing on local actors allows us to consider the discretionary power they can exert and their room for action (agency), which is one of the core issues addressed throughout this book.

1.3 A Methodology Note

This book is based on an analysis of the plurality of action implemented in Milan and Barcelona in the field of municipal policies supporting entrepreneurship. Drawing on the approaches outlined above, it first reconstructs the framework of action taken to support entrepreneurship, partly in an attempt to connect up the individual actions to one another in order to shed light on the policy rationales behind MESPs, as well as the main characteristics adopted in Barcelona and Milan (actors, problem-setting, goal-setting, instruments, target groups, main outcomes, contradictions and conflicts) and their local specificities. The book then seeks to enquire into the way in which policy actors—including beneficiaries—interpret, invalidate, replicate and contest neoliberal views on entrepreneurship support policies and the ideal models of individual subjectivity and urban governance marshalled as pivotal elements in "start-up urbanism". Finally, the study questions the implications of MESPs in relation to the distribution of risks and opportunities between beneficiaries.

These objectives were pursued through qualitative research methods and techniques and multi-site fieldwork. The study's data was collected between January 2017 and May 2018 using primarily semi-structured and open-ended interviews in Barcelona and Milan. Limiting the research to just two cities allowed for in-depth analysis enabling both the diversity of programmes promoted to foster entrepreneurship in both contexts and the perspectives of the various policy actors, including the beneficiaries, to be considered. Once the programmes adopted and the organisations

[3] At the horizontal level, governance has been defined as "a negotiation mechanism for formulating and implementing policy that actively seeks the involvement of stake-holders and civil society organisations besides government bodies and experts" (García, 2006, p. 745).

involved had been mapped I interviewed sixty-five people: thirty-one were key stakeholders and thirty-four were young people supported by the programmes mapped. Indeed, as far as the beneficiaries are concerned, I decided to focus on only one of the main target groups (the most privileged), namely young people under the age of 35.[4] The purpose was to "bind the case", a procedure often recommended to "ensure that your study remains reasonable in scope" (Baxter & Jack, 2008, p. 546). In these interviews specific attention was paid to the beneficiaries' biographies, the circumstances within which the decision to go into business developed, the explicit motives behind the entrepreneurial choices made, any labour market experiences, differing ways of experiencing entrepreneurship, the meanings young beneficiaries attached to entrepreneurship, the role played by the programme they were involved in, representations of the issues at stake, perceived risks and opportunities and the characteristics of entrepreneurial projects. The interviews were conducted in Italian and Spanish and were anonymous (invented names were used to avoid depersonalisation while maintaining anonymity). To stimulate discussion with young people and recapture their attention towards the end of interviews which often lasted more than an hour, I asked them their impressions of two newspaper articles for each case applauding the heroism of entrepreneurs and celebrating young entrepreneurs' initiative, sometimes in juxtaposition with peers portrayed as "bamboccioni",[5] to use an Italian term employed in one the articles selected (Fig. 1.1 and 1.2).

Before embarking on conversations with the young beneficiaries, I sometimes spoke of my own experience setting up a social enterprise, attempting to briefly outline this in neutral tones conveying neither positive nor negative appraisal. This, I feel, contributed to building a rapport. Interviews were recorded with the prior consent of respondents, transcribed and analysed using thematic analysis techniques backed by qualitative data analysis software (NVivo). The qualitative data was examined using both deductive and inductive approaches.

[4] This age limit was initially chosen in accordance with the late transition to adulthood particularly prevalent among young people in southern contexts. Subsequently, policy actors confirmed the particular relevance of young adults (aged 30–35) to youth entrepreneurship in both contexts and in the programmes implemented.

[5] This is a colloquial term used to describe young adults who come across as over-dependent on parents or delay adulthood by engaging in limited responsibility behaviours.

Altroché bamboccioni, giovani attratti da impresa

Uno su 3 si sente pronto da subito a creare un'azienda

06 ottobre, 21:16

ROMA - I giovani italiani non sono tutti bamboccioni: uno su 3 si sente pronto da subito a fare impresa. Il 33% si dice infatti "molto o abbastanza preparato" a creare un'azienda. Emerge da un'indagine Swg per Legacoop sul pianeta under 35. Non sognano il posto fisso: al 49% piacerebbe avviare un'impresa se solo ne avesse la possibilità. Scuola e università però centrano poco, conta di più la voglia di fare (53%). Troppi i vegliardi in Parlamento e istituzioni: più giovani garantirebbero più meritocrazia ed efficienza.

1 di 1 Guarda la foto

Giovani alla ricerca del lavoro

Vent enni d'Italia, gli «startupperoi»

La Rete, il coraggio di buttarsi e un'idea diversa dalle altre: quelli che creano il loro posto di lavoro

(Afp)

Il loro motto è: non c'è il posto di lavoro? Il mio me lo creo da solo. Ma, se li cercate, trovarli non è facile: non sono sulle Pagine Gialle. Non sono gli avatar professionali di genitori che li raccomandano, né di network universitari che li promuovono. Paradossalmente

Fig. 1.1 Visual-text stimuli used during interviews with youth policy beneficiaries in Italy[6]

[6] The article, "Altro che bamboccioni, un giovane su tre si sente pronto a creare un'impresa da subito" (What *bamboccioni? One in three young people feel ready to set up a business right away*), is available at: http://www.ansa.it/web/notizie/rubriche/economia/2012/10/06/Altroche-bamboccioni-giovani-attratti-impresa_7589470.html (latest access: 21 April 2023). The article "Vent'enni d'Italia, gli startupperoi" (*Italy's 20-year-olds, its start-up heroes*), is available at: https://www.corriere.it/economia/12_marzo_11/sideri-gli-startupperoi_b28d411a-6b4d-11e1-a02c-63a438fc3a4e.shtml (latest access: 21 April 2023).

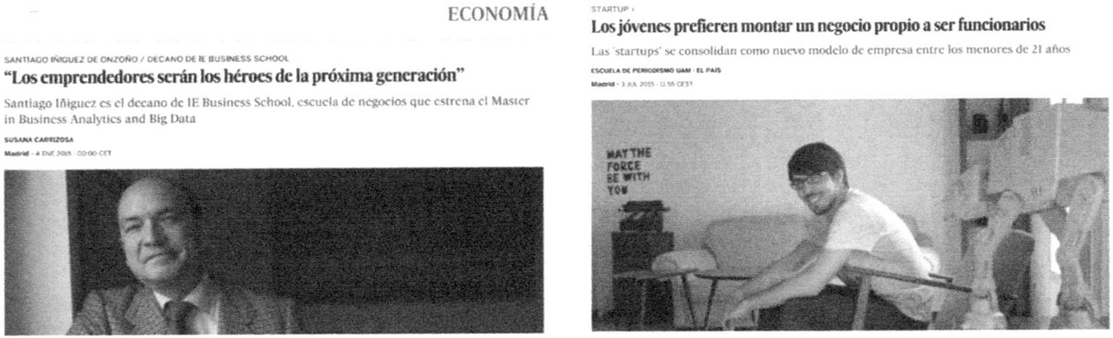

Fig. 1.2 Visual-text stimuli used during interviews with youth policy beneficiaries in Spain[7]

[7] The article "Los emprendedores serán los héroes de la próxima generación" (*Entrepreneurs will be the heroes of the next generation*), is available at: https://elpais.com/economia/2014/12/30/actualidad/1419953210_882613.html (latest access: 21 April 2023). The article "Los jovenes prefieren montar un negocio propio a ser funcionarios" (*Young people prefer setting up their own business to becoming officials*), is available at: https://elpais.com/elpais/2015/06/25/masterdeperiodismo/1435222761_235721.html (latest access: 21 April 2023).

The study was also based on documentary analysis (especially annual reports published in Barcelona in the 2010–2017 period, and occasional reports submitted from 2011 to 2017 in Milan). Where samplings are concerned, the research adopted a non-probability sample strategy commonplace in qualitative studies (Ritchie et al., 2003). More to the point, it relied on stakeholder sampling to access the points of view of those involved in designing, supplying or administering the programme or service observed, but also those in receipt of it, such as beneficiaries. Furthermore, a stratified logic was adopted for people selection, to vary the type of programme/measure in which they were involved and to account for the MESPs diversity that emerged during fieldwork.

On this research design basis, this book's aim is to contribute to an informed and nuanced analysis of municipal entrepreneurship support policies.

1.4 The Structure of the Book

The book is structured as follows. This first opening chapter has set out the book's main themes and aims and provided a brief overview of the theories informing the study presented in the following chapters and taking stock of the gaps in the literature. It has also provided certain insights into its research design. Chapter 2 is entitled *"This Is Like a Big Transatlantic Liner": Contingent Converging Trends* and explores the economic, social, political and cultural context in which the start-up city emerged and found its way into the discourses and political practices of local actors in Barcelona and Milan. The argument presented here is that convergence dynamics—leading to MESP patterns aligned with neoliberal models of intervention and governance—are at work in the two cities, against the backdrop of the transition to the "post-Fordist city", but in accordance with very different timescales, modalities, governance models and characteristics. This chapter highlights the multilevel and multifactorial dynamics at work with a special focus on the historical and institutional legacies, culture, political paradigms and socio-economic characteristics of the two local contexts. Chapter 3, *Inclusive Entrepreneurship Policies: Reproducing Heterogeneity, Negotiating Ambivalence*, examines the Schumpeterian view of entrepreneurship prevalent in the start-up city rhetoric, taking a closer look at entrepreneurship programme implementation and outcomes in the context of MESPs and the emergence of "inclusive" approaches to entrepreneurship support policies. Furthermore, it highlights the heterogeneity and ordinariness underlying the fashionable start-up city label, discussing the ambivalence implicit in this heterogeneity and the way in which local actors negotiate views and strategies on problems and emerging contradictions to be addressed. Chapter 4 is entitled *"The Mindset Has Changed a Lot"? Situated Agency of Youth Entrepreneurs* and provides insights into MESPs in Barcelona and Milan from the perspective of their young beneficiaries, by analysing their experiences, the motives behind their decisions to become entrepreneurs and their own experiences and representations of entrepreneurship. As well as highlighting the discourse, symbol and practice standardisation processes at work the chapter also examine the way young beneficiaries resignify the entrepreneurial device within their self-fulfilment strategies. The fifth chapter is entitled *Differentiated Inclusion* and focuses on the ambivalence inherent in inclusiveness as a guiding principle of entrepreneurship support policies. In particular the chapter discusses the danger of unequal risk and opportunity distribution between young beneficiaries, especially along the "innovative" and "ordinary" youth dividing line, and highlights the main dynamics of "differentiated inclusion" generated by the simultaneous interaction of differentiated and differentiating policy instruments and pre-existing inequalities in a highly individualised context. Chapter 6 draws a number of conclusions.

References

Ahl, H., & Marlow, S. (2021). Exploring the false promise of entrepreneurship through a postfeminist critique of the enterprise policy discourse in Sweden and the UK. *Human Relations, 74*(1), 41–68.

Amin, A., & Thrift, N. (1992). Neo-marshallian nodes in global networks. *International Journal of Urban and Regional Research, 6*(4), 571–587.

Bagnasco, A. (1977). *Tre Italie: la problematica territoriale dello sviluppo italiano.* il Mulino.

Bagnasco, A., & Le Galès, P. (2000). *Cities in contemporary Europe.* Cambridge University Press.

Barbieri, P., & Bison, I. (2004). Self-employment in Italy: Scaling the class barriers. In R. Arum & W. Müller (Eds.), *The reemergence of self-employment: A comparative study of self-employment dynamics and social inequalities* (pp. 310–347). Princeton University Press.

Baxter, P., & Jack, S. (2008). Qualitative case study methodology: Study design and implementation for novice researchers. *The Qualitative Report, 13*(4), 544–559.

Becattini, G. (2002). From Marshall's to the Italian "industrial districts". A brief critical reconstruction. In A. Q. Curzio & M. Fortis (Eds.), *Complexity and industrial clusters. Contributions to economics* (pp. 83–106). Physica-Verlag HD.

Beck, U. (1992). *Risk society: Towards a new modernity*. Sage.

Beck, U., & Beck-Gernsheim, E. (2002). *Individualization: Institutionalized individualism and its social and political consequences*. Sage.

Bifulco, L. (2012). Melinda e Melinda. Note su partecipazione, agency e capacità di aspirare. In O. De Leonardis & M. Deriu (Eds.), *Il Futuro nel Quotidiano. Studi Sociologici sulla Capacità di Aspirare*. Egea.

Bifulco, L. (2017). *Social policies and public action*. Routledge.

Bifulco, L., & Mozzana, C. (2016). Introduzione: oltre l'employability. Approcci e prospettive per le transizioni giovanili scuola-lavoro. *Sociologia del lavoro, 141*(1), 7–22.

Boltanski, L., Thévenot, L. (2006). On Justification. Princeton, NJ: Princeton University Press.

Borelli, G. (2012). La politica economica urbana. Teorie e modi di governance. Carocci.

Borghi, V. (2011). One-way Europe? Institutional guidelines, emerging regimes of justification, and paradoxical turns in European welfare capitalism. *European Journal of Social Theory, 3*, 321–341.

Brenner, N. (2004). *New state spaces. Urban governance and the rescaling of statehood*. Oxford University Press.

Brenner, N., Peck, J., Theodore, N., (2010). Variegated neoliberalization: geographies, modalities, pathways. *Global Networks, 10*(2), 182–222.

Bröckling, U. (2016). *The entrepreneurial self: Fabricating a new type of subject*. Sage.

Burroni, L., & Trigilia, C. (2011). *Le città dell'innovazione. Dove e perchè cresce l'alta tecnologia in Italia*. il Mulino.

Camagni, R. (2002). On the concept of territorial competitiveness: Sound or misleading? *Urban Studies, 39*(13), 2395–2411.

Caraher, K., & Reuter, E. (2017). Vulnerability of the "entrepreneurial self": Analysing the interplay between labour markets and social policy. *Social Policy and Society, 163*, 483–496.

Castel, R. (2004). *L'insicurezza sociale. Che significa essere protetti?* Einaudi.

Castel, R. (2016). The rise of uncertainties. *Critical Horizons, 17*(2), 160–167.

Crespo, E., & Serrano, A. P. (2004). The EU's concept of activation for young people: towards a new social contract? In *Are activation policies converging in Europe? The European employment strategy for young people* (pp. 13–46). European Trade Union Institute.

Crouch, C., Le Galès, P., Trigilia, C., & Voelzkow, H. (2004). *Changing governance of local economies*. Oxford University Press.

Cucca, R., & Ranci, C. (2017). *Unequal cities: The challenge of post-industrial transition in times of austerity*. Routledge.
Davies, J. S., & Blanco, I. (2017). Austerity urbanism: Patterns of neo-liberalisation and resistance in six cities of Spain and the UK. *Environment and Planning A, 49*(7), 1517–1536.
Enright, T., et al. (2018). Cities in global capitalism. *The AAG Review of Books, 6*(1), 59–75.
Essers, C., Dey, P., Tedmanson, D., Verduyn, K. (2017). *Critical Perspectives on Entrepreneurship. Challenging Dominant Discourses*. Routledge.
Eurocities. (2013). *Cities supporting inclusive entrepreneurship*. Eurocities.
European Commission. (2016). *The state of European cities 2016*. Publications Office of the European Union.
Evans, K. (2002). Taking control of their lives? Agency in young adult transitions in England and the new Germany. *Journal of Youth Studies, 5*(3), 245–269.
Fiorentino, S. (2018, May). Re-making urban economic geography. Start-ups, entrepreneurial support and the makers movement: A critical assessment of policy mobility in Rome. *Geoforum, 93*, 116–119.
Le Galès, P. (2002). *European cities: Social conflicts and governance*. Oxford University Press.
Le Galès, P. (2016). Neoliberalism and urban change: Stretching a good idea too far? *Territory, Politics, Governance, 4*(2), 154–172.
Le Galès, P. (2018). Urban political economy beyond convergence: Robust but differentiated unequal European cities. In A. Andreotti, D. Benassi, & Y. Kazepov (Eds.), *Western capitalism in transition* (pp. 217–236). Manchester University Press.
Gallino, L. (1978). *Dizionario di Sociologia*. Utet.
García, M. (2006). Citizenship practices and urban governance in European cities. *Urban Studies, 43*(4), 745–765.
GEM. (2018). *Global report 2017–18, Global Entrepreneurship Monitor*. https://www.gemconsortium.org/report
Hall, P. A. (1993). Policy paradigms, social learning, and the state: The case of economic policymaking in Britain. *Comparative Politics, 25*(3), 275–296.
Harvey, D. (1989). From Managerialism to Entrepreneurialism: The Transformation in Urban Governance in Late Capitalism, *Geografiska Annaler: Series B Human Geography, 71*(1), 3–17.
Harvey, D. (1993). *La crisi della modernità*. il Saggiatore.
Houston, D., & Reuschke, D. (2017). City economies and microbusiness growth. *Urban Studies, 54*(14), 3199–3217.
Jessop, B. (2004). Critical semiotic analysis and cultural political economy. *Critical Discourse Studies, 1*(2), 159–174.
Jessop, B. (2010). Cultural political economy and critical policy studies. *Critical Policy Studies, 3*(3–4), 336–356.

Jessop, B., & Sum, N. L. (2001). Pre-disciplinary and post-disciplinary perspectives. *New Political Economy, 6*, 89–101.

Jessop, B., & Sum, N. L. (2010). Cultural political economy: Logics of discovery, epistemic fallacies, the complexity of emergence, and the potential of the cultural turn. *New Political Economy, 15*(3), 445–451.

Katz, C. (2004). *Growing up global. Economic restructuring and children's everyday lives*. University of Minnesota Press.

Kazepov, Y., Barberis, E., Cucca, R., & Mocca, E. (2022). *Handbook on urban social policies*. Edward Elgar.

Kazepov, Y., Cucca, R., Ahn, B., & Verrier, C. (2021). European cities between continuity and change. In *Companion to urban and regional studies* (pp. 109–134). Wiley-Blackwell.

Keating, M. (2017). The territorial state. In D. King & P. Le Galès (Eds.), *Reconfiguring European states in crisis*. Oxford University Press.

Lascoumes, P., & Le Galès, P. (2012). *Sociologie de l'action publique* (2nd ed.). Armand Colin.

Levenda, A. M., & Tretter, E. (2020). The environmentalization of urban entrepreneurialism: From technopolis to start-up city. *Environment and Planning A, 52*(3), 490–509.

Lodigiani, R., & Scippa, E. (2014). Il self-employment tra politiche del lavoro e occupazionali, nella prospettiva europea dell'attivazione. In P. A. Varesi & A. Vergani (Eds.), *Self-employment e sostegno pubblico all'imprenditorialità* (pp. 227–266). Franco Angeli.

McNeill, D. (2017). Start-ups and the entrepreneurial city. *City, 21*(2), 232–239.

Mind the Bridge. (2018). *Startup city. Hubs in Europe*. Mind the Bridge.

Mingione, E. (2018). The double movement and the perspectives of contemporary capitalism. In A. Andreotti, D. Benassi, & Y. Kazepov (Eds.), *Western capitalism in transition. Global processes, local challenges*. Manchester University Press.

Moini, G. (2013). *Interpretare l'azione pubblica*. Carocci.

Moisio, S., & Rossi, U. (2020). The start-up state: Governing urbanised capitalism. *EPA: Economy and Space, 52*(3), 532–552.

Nico, M., & Caetano, A. (2021). *Structure and agency in young people's lives*. Routledge.

OECD/European Commission. (2017). *The Missing Entrepreneurs 2017. Policies for inclusive entrepreneurship*. OECD Publishing.

OECD/European Union (2017). *The Missing Entrepreneurs 2017: Policies for Inclusive Entrepreneurship*, OECD Publishing.

Paci, M. (2005). *Nuovi lavori, nuovo welfare*. il Mulino.

Panichella, N. (2013). Per scelta o per costrizione? La decisione di mettersi in proprio in tempo di crisi. *Sociologia del lavoro, 131*, 104–119.

Peck, J. (2014). Entrepreneurial urbanism: Between uncommon sense and dull compulsion. *Geografiska Annaler, Series B: Human Geography, 96*(4), 396–401.

Perren, L., Jennings, P. L. (2005). Government Discourses on Entrepreneurship: Issues of Legitimization Subjugation and Power. *Entrepreneurship Theory and Practice, 29*(2), 173–184.

Peters, M. (2001). Education, enterprise culture and the entrepreneurial self: A Foucauldian perspective. *Journal of Educational Enquiry, 2*(2), 58–71.

Pinson, G. (2022). *La città Neoliberale*. Mimesis.

Pinson, G., & Morel Journel, C. (2017). *Debating the neoliberal city*. Routledge.

Pollio, A. (2020). Making the silicon cape of Africa: Tales, theories and the narration of startup urbanism. *Urban Studies, 57*(13), 2715–2732.

Pradel, M., Cano-Hila, A. B., & García, M. (2020). *Urban governance and social innovation. Citizenship, civil society and social movements*. Edward Elgar.

Pradel, M., & García, M. (2021). Policies and policy approaches in cities. In *Companion to urban and regional studies* (pp. 539–561). Wiley-Blackwell.

Ranci, C., Brandsen, T., & Sabatinelli, S. (2014). *Social vulnerability in European cities. The role of local welfare in times of crisis*. Palgrave.

Reynolds, P. D., & Curtin, R. T. (2007). *Panel study of entrepreneurial dynamics program rationale and description*. University of Michigan.

Reynolds, P., Niels, B., Autio, E., Hunt, S., De Bono, N., Servais, I., Lopez-Garcia, P., & Chin, N. (2005). Global Entrepreneurship Monitor: Data collection design and implementation 1998–2003. *Small Business Economics, 24*, 205–231.

Rhodes, R. (2007). Understanding governance: Ten years on. *Organization Studies, 28*(8), 1243–1264.

Ritchie, J., Lewis, J., Nicholls, C. M., & Ormston, R. (2003). *Qualitative research practice. A guide for social science students and researchers*. Sage.

Rossi, U. (2017). *Cities in global capitalism*. Polity Press.

Rossi, U., & Di Bella, A. (2017). Start-up urbanism: New York, Rio de Janeiro and the global urbanization of technology-based economies. *Environment and Planning A, 49*(5), 999–1018.

Sabel, C. (1994). Flexible specialisation and the re-emergence of regional economies. In A. Amin (Ed.), *Post-Fordism: A reader* (pp. 101–156). Blackwell.

Sassen, S. (2006). *Cities in a world economy*. Pine Forge Press.

Schumpeter, J. A. (1947). The creative response in economic history. *The Journal of Economic History, 7*(2), 149–159.

Scott, W. R. (2014). *Institutions and organizations: Ideas, interests, and identities* (4th ed.). Sage.

Serrano Pascual, A., & Martín Martín, P. (2017). From “employab-ility” to “entrepreneurial-ity” in Spain: Youth in the spotlight in times of crisis. *Journal of Youth Studies, 20*(7), 798–821.

Sheehan, M., & Namara, A. M. (2015). *Business start-ups and youth self-employment: A policy literature review synthesis report* (STYLE Working Papers, WP7.1). CROME. University of Brighton.

Simpson, I. (2021). *Cultural political economy of the start-up societies imaginary*. McGill University.

Spanò, A. (2017). *I giovani del Sud di fronte alla crisi*. Franco Angeli.

Spanò, A. (2019). Giovani e lavoro: cambiamenti dei significati del lavoro in tempo di crisi. *Sociologia del lavoro, 154*(2), 203–222.

Sternberg, C. (2023). *Neoliberal urban governance. Spaces, culture and discourses in Buenos Aires and Chicago*. Palgrave Macmillan.

Streeck, W. (2014). The politics of public debt: Neoliberalism, capitalist development and the restructuring of the state. *German Economic Review, 15*(1), 143–165.

Sum, N. L. (2009). The production of hegemonic policy discourses: “Competitiveness” as a knowledge brand and its (re-)contextualizations. *Critical Policy Studies, 3*(2), 184–203.

Threadgold, S., Farrugia, D., & Coffey, J. (2021). Challenging the structure/agency binary. In M. Nico & A. Caetano (Eds.), *Structure and agency in young people’s lives* (pp. 15–29). Abingdon: Routledge.

van Berkel, R., & Møller, H. I. (2002). *Active social policies in the EU*. The Policy Press.

Walther, A. (2005). Risks and responsibilities? The individualisation of youth transitions and the ambivalence between participation and activation in Europe. *Social Work and Society, 3*(1), 116–127.

Woodman, D., & Vanderharst, A. (2021). Reflexivity in late modernity. Understanding young lives in the context of social change. In M. Nico & A. Caetano (Eds.), *Structure and agency in young people’s lives* (pp. 201–215). Routledge.

CHAPTER 2

"This Is Like a Big Transatlantic Liner": Contingent Converging Trends

Abstract This chapter takes the reader into the economic, social, political and cultural contexts in which the start-up city emerged and found its way into the discourses and public actions in Barcelona, Spain and Milan, Italy. The argument presented here is that convergence dynamics—leading to MESP patterns aligned with neoliberal models of intervention and governance—are at work in the two cities, against the backdrop of the transition to the "post-Fordist city", but in accordance with very different timescales, modalities, governance models and characteristics. This chapter highlights the multilevel and multifactorial dynamics at work with a special focus on the historical and institutional legacies, culture, policy paradigms and socio-economic characteristics of the two local contexts.

Keywords Municipal entrepreneurship support policies · Neoliberal urban governance · Barcelona · Milan · Start-up city · Local embeddedness · Variegated neoliberalisation

> Any serious attempt to address the economic crisis, increase the employment rate and lift citizens out of poverty must put entrepreneurship at its heart. (…) Cities can provide ideal start-up community environments where inclusive entrepreneurship thrives and where innovators want to

M. Dodaro, *Unpacking the 'Start-up City'*,
https://doi.org/10.1007/978-3-031-50212-5_2

> live. Much research points to city-level interventions as the most significant element in building and fostering entrepreneurial ecosystems. City authorities across Europe are doing this. They support start-ups and early-growth businesses in the form of incubators and accelerators. They facilitate the formation of networks and access to these. They raise entrepreneurial awareness and promote links between the public, private and knowledge sectors.
>
> (Chair of the Eurocities Economic Development Forum, Eurocities, 2013, p. 4)

This extract is particularly evocative of the commitment in European cities to supporting entrepreneurship and start-ups in particular since the 2008 crisis. It echoes the idea that entrepreneurship is key to promoting both social inclusion and economic growth, but above all that any movement in this direction cannot be brought to fruition without cities. Yet, it should be underlined that, in common with a wide range of urban programmes and policies, such initiatives are embedded in multilevel dynamics. These unfold vertically—in compliance with the European normative framework, in which entrepreneurship figures prominently in several policy areas, spanning economic development, active labour policies and education—and horizontally, shaped by networks of local and translocal actors via organisations such as Eurocities. This latter is a network of cities (today more than two hundred), founded in 1986 by the mayors of Barcelona, Birmingham, Frankfurt, Lyon, Milan and Rotterdam, whose aims include bringing the network's proposals to the attention of the European Union (advocacy) and sharing EU best practices, funding opportunities and developments.

In addition, processes such as economic rescaling, service rollout, dissemination of new technologies and financial and organisational innovations have contributed in various ways to generating favourable conditions for both "ordinary" and innovative technological and/or digital enterprises. The latter have also been supported by the onset of "platform capitalism" fuelled by investment from venture capital funds and other financial institutions (Arvidsson & Luise, 2019; Charnock & Ribera-Fumaz, 2023; Langley & Leyshon, 2016; Rossi & Di Bella, 2017). A further driver is the rise of neoliberalism and enterprise culture (Chapter 1) recently reinvigorated by the "Californian ideology" embodied by successful digital age entrepreneurs from Steve Jobs to Mark Zuckerberg, "a new entrepreneurial creed that instils a new enthusiasm for the creation of highly innovative and potentially profitable entrepreneurial activities in young students, knowledge workers, policy stakeholders and financial investors, and whose mission is to change the world" (Luise, 2019, p. 9, author's translation).

However, policies whose purpose is to foster entrepreneurial attitudes and new businesses stand out for their heterogeneity and ambivalence, attributes that are specific to entrepreneurship and often denote everything and nothing, from street vendors to digital entrepreneurs. I will examine this heterogeneity further in the following chapters but it is significant that this complexity has often been eclipsed by representations centring on the innovative and technological nature of start-ups. The phenomenon is greatly on the rise, but its undeniable prominence in the public debate and collective imagination is often independent of its socio-economic relevance or weight in the new firm birth rates and development dynamics. Furthermore, there is a predominant emphasis on the early stages, its inherent value and success stories, often overshadowing factors such as the notably high mortality rate (Arvidsson & Luise, 2019; Chiarello, 2017).

All this notwithstanding, labels such as start-up economy and start-up city are now buzzwords which make them both economic realities and "economic imaginaries" at the same time (Jessop, 2010). The start-up city concept has been marshalled by the majority of recent urban marketing and attractiveness strategies and consensus-building processes around new (post-industrial) symbols, ideas, entrepreneurship conceptions (Aldrich & Ruef, 2018) and entrepreneurial subjectivity models (i.e. autonomous, responsible, self-regulating individuals). It is a label which undoubtedly conjures up specific city visions (e.g. smart, sustainable, innovative, attractive), urban economy, economic development and employment by highlighting the growing relevance and popularity of self-employment in highly individualised labour markets and societies in the context of the knowledge economy. It is partly by leveraging benchmarking reports and indices which rank cities by certain criteria (e.g. the presence of high-tech start-ups, investment, "cultural vibrancy",[1] etc.) that the start-up city has

[1] This is one of the indicators used by the Cultural and Creative Cities Monitor, a tool launched by the European Commission to assess and benchmark European cities, available at: https://composite-indicators.jrc.ec.europa.eu/cultural-creative-cities-monitor/performance-map (accessed: 13 June 2023).

entered the best practices pantheon, determining the metrics and standards by which city success is to be judged. The start-up city concept also exemplifies an urban branding strategy that—as D'Ovidio (2016) argued on the subject of the comparable "creative city" label—constructs and promotes "the *right* image of the city", i.e. an image that is "functional to increasing international competition" and "appealing for the global marketing, and for the attractiveness of the city". Image construction of this sort, D'Ovidio explains, centres around selecting some of the "core values" specific to each city which "city brand builders" want to their identities and futures to be associated with. To this end, they adopt a "selective storytelling" strategy in which certain urban dimensions are emphasised at the expense of others, contributing to promoting and justifying certain urban policies over others (pp. 32–33). Two points are worth emphasising in this regard. The first is that these dynamics contribute to signifying local practices while building consensus and/or masking tensions. The second is that they are rooted in symbolic and material processes bound up with the various economic and social changes at work in cities over the last forty years in the shift from the Fordist to the post-Fordist city. The next section explores the economic, social, political and cultural context in which the start-up city concept emerged and made its way into the discourses and political practices of local actors in Barcelona and Milan to account for the long-term trajectory underlying the growing importance of MESPs.

2.1 MESPs: Multi-scalar and Multi-dimensional Trajectories

The form taken by municipal entrepreneurship support policies (MESPs) in Barcelona and Milan has varied significantly in time frame, functioning method and pattern terms. Such policies are the product of contingent convergence processes which, on the one hand, rely on shared representations and trends which contribute concretely feasible and legitimate potential scenarios and, on the other hand, culminate into some extent divergent outcomes dependent on contextual specificities and the social action taken.

To begin with, the economic, social, political and cultural characteristics of the two cities are essential to understanding the emergence and evolution of their urban entrepreneurship policies. Both are medium-sized cities and capitals of two high-income regions, Lombardy and

Catalonia, respectively. They outperform their countries on a number of fronts, such as economic growth, employment trends and education levels. OECD data for their functional urban areas shows that in 2019—prior to the pandemic—per capita gross domestic product was EUR 45,431 in Barcelona and EUR 50,127 in Milan (respectively 13% and 12.8% of GDP).[2] This is an important wealth indicator, but it tells us nothing about how this is distributed or created. The sector which contributes most to this GDP is the service branch, whose expansion has left its mark on the transition to post-Fordism that has variously shaped European cities in recent decades. This is especially the case of former industrial cities such as Barcelona and Milan, which have deindustrialised significantly since the late 1970s, although industry is still a significant presence in both (Cucca & Maestripieri, 2017). The Catalonia autonomous community has seen Spain's most significant industrial development. In 2021, industry generated 20.3% of the region's total gross added value, outperforming that of Spain as a whole (17%) and bringing the region closer to EU levels (20.2%) (Barcelona Activa, 2022). Lombardy is the Italy's number one manufacturing region and one of Europe's most important, accounting for a fifth of Italian GDP and a quarter of its exports (Assolombarda, 2021). The integration of the two cities into their broader regional contexts shows a less clear-cut watershed between Fordism and post-Fordism than many analyses have suggested.

However, within the two administrative cities' boundaries the de-industrialisation process has been massive and its economic, social and spatial—and also symbolic—impact significant. Several sites previously associated with industrialisation have become emblems of crisis, abandonment and decay (Rossi & Vanolo, 2010). The transition to the tertiary sector has thus also been a shift to new symbols and images of the city, the urban economy and its inhabitants and workers (D'Ovidio, 2016). Sassen (2007) highlighted that representations of this kind emphasise the tertiary economy's wealthier economic sectors and professional profiles, concealing the flip side of the coin, such as low value-added services. Examples include sectors such as food and accommodation, care and transport, namely crucial sectors of the urban economy often

[2] Data extracted on 15 September 2023 from OECD.Stat. Data reported is the most recent pre-pandemic data. However, the economic weight of the two cities in their national economies was not diminished by the socio-economic impact of the pandemic, as this data source shows.

associated with demand for low-skilled labour and insecure working conditions (e.g. low wages, seasonal and short-term contracts) (Cucca & Maestripieri, 2017). Overall economic dynamicity has eclipsed the emergence of new socio-spatial inequalities and the growing tension between competitiveness and social justice objectives (Cucca & Ranci, 2017). The start-up city discourse has similarly emphasised a specific representation of entrepreneurship and related urban policies consistent with images of a post-Fordist creative, innovative and competitive city, albeit with certain important differences between Barcelona and Milan, as we will see below.

2.1.1 Milan: Cultivating the Entrepreneurial Ethos

Beginning in the 1980s, Milan gradually consolidated its status as international capital of fashion and design and home to many sector companies and schools, as well as to large-scale related events (e.g. Milan Fashion Week, Salone Internazionale del Mobile). Hosting the Italian Stock Exchange means that Milan is also an important financial centre with all that this entails for the proliferation of finance-related companies, such as business consulting and legal services. It is also home to health and biomedical research, high value-added business services, higher education and training with eight universities and many research institutions, advertising and sport (notably soccer). Milan is an important publishing centre in Italy, and a number of nationally important magazines, televisions and radio stations are based here. It also provides a significant number of cultural and tourist services and goods. A great many small businesses have also sprung up around these economic segments, and in the tertiary sector in general, contributing to shaping Milan's image as an innovation, creativity and entrepreneurship hub (Armondi & Di Vita, 2018; Mugnano et al., 2010).

The city's economic dynamism has been facilitated by plural governance in which a range of actors play an important part, including the Chamber of Commerce which has sponsored synergies with a number of academic institutions. Other influential players include trade unions, employer associations such as Assolombarda (a local business association) and banking foundations. As Andreotti and Le Galès (2019) have pointed out, the flip side of this economic dynamism coin is Milan's ambiguous relationship with its political dimension, encapsulated in the words of city mayor Albertini (1997–2006) who described himself as "a condominium administrator" and those of current mayor, Giuseppe Sala, who argued that "Milan has no time to wait for politics" and that the city "does not want to be steered or spurred on" (p. 11). Milan is often depicted as a "self-governing city" characterised by weak public regulation and a lack of strong local political leadership and governance networks "able to produce resources and projects built without (and sometimes against) the public administration" (Pasqui, 2018, p. 135). Its economic success is the result of what Mugnano et al. (2010, p. 249) refer to as a bottom-up strategy driven by private entrepreneurial initiatives and a laissez-faire policy approach (Mingione et al., 2007). The decentralisation processes that followed legislative action in Italy from the early 2000s onwards have, to some extent, expanded the local public room for manoeuvre, but local governance has remained relatively weak and fragmented, characterised by flagship projects and the primacy of private economic interests (see also Cottacin & Zimmerman, 2016).

However, this weakness in governance is in some sense functional to Milan's positive narrative, which has grown up around the "moral capital" of Italy myth (Mingione et al., 2007) characterised by an emphasis on work ethic, understood as a primary source of social inclusion, and economic success (Andreotti & Le Galès, 2019). The moral traits most frequently emphasised in the public discourse are entrepreneurial mindset, a propensity for hard work and the self-made-man and competition ideologies (Guerrini, 2017; Rosa, 2009). These project an idea of Milan as the main master of its own destiny but also as a sort of economic and cultural leader for the country as a whole. Its implicit exaltation of the competitive, self-sacrificing and entrepreneurial spirit contributes to shaping the symbolic universe in which the actions of its stakeholders, as well as its policies and instruments, take on meaning. This cultural climate was partially mitigated by the city's welfare system until the 1990s, a system set up post-World War II and named "Ambrosian" after the city's patron saint. This was shaped by social, reformist Catholicism designed to strengthen social citizenship and social equity, as well as public governance, direct management of services and cooperation with the city's social stakeholders (Benassi, 2019). However, since the 1990s, in line with a more generalised crisis of the European welfare state, residualisation and a shift towards market-oriented approaches (Costa et al., 2016) have been the order of the day. The moral capital concept has, to some extent, been undermined by other events, especially by judicial enquiries in the 1990s which brought to light widespread corruption both political and corporate in Italy as a whole, but with Milan itself in pole position. But the image has survived and frequently crops up in the national press and public discourse. In the interviews for this study, the city's entrepreneurial policies were described as an opportunity to enhance and "indulge [...] the ethos of the private, i.e. the entrepreneurial ethos of the whole city", and as something of an imperative mission for Milan, rhetorically represented as "responsible for showing the social and economic way. This has always been the case and cannot, at this stage be overturned. The time has really come to say 'let's change and try to innovate. If Milan can't do it who can?'" (Urban Economy and Employment Directorate, Milan Municipality, February 2017).

The city's 2011 elections marked a meaningful watershed, with the victory of a centre-left coalition bringing a long period of centre-right government lasting from 1993 to an end (the centre-left then won again in 2016 and 2021). Several scholars see this centre-left phase as an attempt to strengthen local government's leadership capacity and the participatory governance dimension, and to channel socio-economic development in the direction of greater inclusiveness, including through municipal entrepreneurship support policies (Torri, 2017). This was implemented while the city was preparing to host the 2015 World Expo, another particularly significant moment for Milan. The Expo helped reinvigorate Milan's national and international appeal (including as both a business and tourist destination) and rebranded its "Milan model" image (Andreotti & Le Galès, 2019). As Moisio and Rossi (2020) have noted, in 2016 then-Prime Minister Matteo Renzi commented on the event to the effect that "Milan has to take Italy by the hand and show the way forward out of a challenging situation affecting our country at the economic level". Not surprisingly, then, Expo commissioner Giuseppe Sala was later elected mayor (2016–ongoing), reflecting the mega-event's importance. The Expo has also drawn attention to youth entrepreneurship, innovation and green start-ups, and provided significant new business creation incentives (Milan Chamber of Commerce, 2015).

2.1.2 *The Barcelona Model of Entrepreneurialism*

Barcelona's economic, social and spatial characteristics have changed significantly since the city bid to host the 1992 Olympic Games in the late 1980s. The urban economy has seen radical transformation, leading to sustained growth in gross domestic product, modernised services and the urban environment, housing improvements and a general raising of city living standards (Degen & García, 2012). Economically speaking, Barcelona has transitioned from industrial (in crisis) to post-industrial city and expanded its services (Pareja-Eastaway & Pradel, 2015; Trullén, 2002). In 2018, its leading economic sectors included business services (27.5%), retail trade (17.2%), education, health and social services (10.2%), real estate (8.2%), construction (8.1%) and the hospitality sector (6.1%) (Barcelona Activa, 2020). Barcelona has also made a name for itself as an international metropolis and one of Europe's most economically dynamic areas (Trullén, 2002). In particular, expanded air, motorway and rail connections and port renovation have contributed to making it one of southern Europe's most important trade hubs (Gentile, 2011). Exports and foreign investment have also increased, making it an important economic and business centre. It has undergone an intense economic tertiarisation process (Trullén, 2002) and actively promoted the tourism, cultural and leisure economic sectors to boost urban attractiveness and competitiveness (García & Judd, 2012), contributing to making it one of the world's primary tourist destinations, raising significant concerns regarding the socio-spatial inequalities this entails.

Barcelona has eight universities as well as a great many technology and research centres and its public institutions play an active part in shaping this urban economic structure through local development plans, together with the private sector. The 1992 Olympic Games, in particular, attracted corporate interest in public policy. Blakeley (2010) contended that public–private partnerships (the latter mainly businesses) were facilitated, on the one hand, by the growing responsiveness of business elites to all policies capable of enhancing the city's economic attractiveness and competitiveness and, on the other, by a strategy designed to overcome the city's growing budgetary constraints by increasing endogenous resources and renovate its obsolete industrial spaces (Degen & García, 2012). Barcelona's 1985 Strategic Economic and Social Plan drawn up to enable the city to meet the challenge of hosting the Olympic Games set up public-led partnerships with private stakeholders as the governance model of choice (Cano-Hila et al., 2017; Degen & García, 2012). During this period, a number of the traits adopted in city governance were typical of urban entrepreneurialism, institutionalising strategic planning and introducing marketing and urban competitiveness strategies, while retaining a focus on the social cohesion and strong public leadership characteristic of the "Barcelona model". In fact, "the lesson to learn from Barcelona's way of making and conceiving the city is that the City Council has always been the key actor in managing the process of urban change. While it certainly has adopted a more entrepreneurial approach, the public sector has, so far, always steered the governance and decision- making processes of the city" (Degen & García, 2012, p. 1034). Political stability has ensured some continuity as regards economic and social development targets and plans. Barcelona was governed by leftist coalitions from 1979 to 2011, which also benefited from closer cooperation with the regional government from 2003 to 2010, when the latter was also headed by a progressive coalition (Cano-Hila et al., 2017). The solidity of public leadership is also to be contextualised within the consolidation of democracy and state power rescaling processes under way in Spain (Cano-Hila et al., 2017; Degen & García, 2012).

The Olympics enabled a "Barcelona brand" to be built, "the vision for the city during this period was to become world-class with a focus on attracting, growing and retaining talent and creative businesses in the services/knowledge-based sector". The economic imaginary conjures up an economic model "built heavily on knowledge, entrepreneurship and value-added services" (OECD, 2009, p. 16). As one expert on Barcelona's metropolitan strategic plans explained in an interview, it was during this period in particular that the municipality began to think that "the city's primary company was the municipality itself" and that it could become a crucial "revitalizing instrument" for the economy (December 2017). Competitiveness was put on the local agenda and consolidated via the governance model mentioned above. Barcelona deployed strategies to increase its attractiveness to businesses, tourists and the "creative classes" and to foster an economy based on knowledge and technological innovation (Charnock et al., 2013). Crossa et al. (2010) noted that, in this period, "Barcelona profits from the attractiveness of the city, and projects the image of the city as an ideal place for business, to stimulate successful projects, disseminate the results and attract Spanish capital investment into large enterprises" (p. 86).

At the same time, urban and economic renewal has generally gone hand in hand with "the aim of enhancing social cohesion and a sense of belonging to the city" (Degen & García, 2012 p. 1022), strengthened by the Catalan identity and an emphasis on autonomy (Gentile, 2011), together with city's strong social participation tradition (Blakeley, 2005; García, 1993). Citizen and social stakeholder participation (associations, third sector) is another key feature of the Barcelona governance model

(Blakeley, 2005, 2010) which has not averted the growth of independent social movements, including protest groups (Pradel et al., 2020). The importance of the city's social movements is demonstrated by recent political events which have seen some of these movements entering the electoral arena and led to Ada Colau, Platform for People Affected by Mortgages (PAH) activist, being elected mayor of the city from 2015 to 2023. This marked a number of important reversals in relation to the economic and employment development policies undertaken in previous years with their strong focus on competitiveness and entrepreneurship support, especially during the 2011–2015 conservative-led government (Cano-Hila et al., 2017).

Large-scale public investment designed to attract and support new businesses and create a business-friendly environment is the goal of project 22@ which began in 1998. Also known as Distrito 22@, this is an urban renewal project whose goals include the social and economic transformation of the old industrial, working-class neighbourhood of Poblenou, the "Catalan Manchester" (Charnock et al., 2013; Charnock & Ribera-Fumaz, 2023; Crossa et al., 2010; Pareja-Eastaway & Pradel, 2015). The project was put forward as "an economic development project which aims at stimulating the creation of a scientific, technological and cultural pole aimed at becoming one of the main platforms for innovation and knowledge economy in Spain and Europe" (OECD, 2009, p. 38). The 22@Barcelona district has brought in multiple stakeholders and organisations with a view to building an entrepreneurial and innovative "ecosystem" such as cutting edge companies, universities and training centres and research centres making "this district a very attractive place to establish a business and work" (ivi). As Crossa et al. (2010) noted, it was not simply an urban renewal project "but signalled a new form of understanding the city" and aimed "to transform Barcelona into a leading knowledge society, in particular by encouraging new-generation activities related to and requiring education, creativity and innovation" especially in the biomed, energy, design, media and ICT sectors (pp. 86–87). This is the genesis of municipal entrepreneurship support policies, explored in greater detail below.

2.2 The Local Embeddedness of MESPs

Entrepreneurship policies have thus acquired considerable importance in Barcelona and Milan against a backdrop of multilevel and multifactorial dynamics. These have included transitions to post-Fordist cities, the rise of the service economy and the incorporation of entrepreneurial models of governance and action (Harvey, 1989) contributing to reorienting public action for the purposes of increasing cities' attractiveness and competitiveness. More generally, we have seen that this has involved rebuilding cities' economic, social and local identity foundations after the Fordist city crisis, under the new aegis of the knowledge economy, higher value-added services, technology, creativity and innovation. As urban neoliberalisation theories have highlighted, these paradigms have influenced the political priorities of city leaders and contributed to the dissemination of market-oriented policy approaches, often prioritising the needs of the "creative class" (Florida, 2002), i.e. entrepreneur-innovators, designers and professionals of various kinds, as well as growth and competitiveness over redistributive and social justice goals, and responsible and entrepreneurial subjectivity (Brenner, 2004; Peck, 2014; Rossi, 2017; Sternberg, 2023). Within this framework, policies to support entrepreneurship have developed discursively within city branding strategies. At the same time, they have been incorporated into structures, services, programmes, development plans and guidelines by leveraging both symbolic and material resources. These are resources cultural political economists generally see as determining the success of specific economic imaginaries over others. One important resource is persuasive force and an ability to fit in entirely consistently into broader processes alongside other hegemonic economic imaginaries (Jessop, 2004; Jessop & Oosterlynck, 2008) such as, in this case, that of the creative city or the knowledge-based economy.

The next sections outline economic imaginary structuring process, i.e. the way these consolidate by taking shape within complex structures and solid formal and informal relationships which are, for this reason, difficult to change. In the words of one interviewee, it is the way a given class of representations and imaginaries can take shape in "a big transatlantic liner, bearing considerable inertia" (SSE-Social and Solidarity Economy Directorate, Barcelona, April 2018).

2.2.1 *Barcelona Activa: A Publicly Managed MESP Model*

Barcelona Activa (BA) is the city council's local development agency. It was set up in 1986 with the primary task of implementing municipal policies designed to support local economic development, foster the city's attractiveness and competitiveness, stimulate business creation and growth and improve employment levels including via training and skills development (Cano-Hila et al., 2017; Gentile, 2011; OECD, 2009). BA is a municipal capital company (*sociedad mercantil municipal*), a type of body based on the organisational principles of agile management and functional specialisation. These are private entities wholly owned by the city council of Barcelona (the board of directors includes representation from all municipal groups). Local government's political orientation is accordingly of central importance: "as a municipal company, every four years, when municipal elections are held, we are a little... we implement the municipal policy of the specific government in power, and economic policy is bound up with the municipality's economic and political programme" (Entrepreneurship Directorate, BA, October 2017). The European Union's policy guidance also plays an important part in this. BA has always aligned with the main requirements of the European Employment Strategy, especially those concerning vocational training, entrepreneurship and women's participation in the labour market (Cano-Hila et al., 2017).

BA's role has increased, especially since the late 1990s and after 2003. Gentile (2011) has noted this consolidation is the outcome, on the one hand, of decentralisation of responsibility processes in the field of active labour and development policies in the late 1990s and, on the other, of a closer alignment between city and regional governments since 2003, when BA consolidated its structures, action, resource base and management capacity. In fact, the earlier period saw a divergence between the conservatives in the *Generalitat* (more inclined towards greater centralisation and privatisation of development and employment services) and the government in Barcelona (more oriented towards decentralisation in favour of government agencies closer to residents and firms, and collaborative governance at the local level).

In 2010, the election of a conservative government at the Generalitat, together with austerity policies, contributed to a significant decrease in BA's budget. An analysis of the annual reports shows that the Catalan government provided over fifty per cent of BA's entire budget in 2011.

In the years which followed, the proportion of funds allocated by the Catalan government within the total budget decreased sharply, increasing the already significant municipal contribution (43% of the total budget available in 2011) by 32 percentage points in 2017 (75% of the total budget). Nonetheless, after the first major reduction in available funds in 2012, the budget increased steadily in the years which followed, from 42 million Euros in 2011 to 54.6 million Euros in 2017, with more funds being set aside for employment services than entrepreneurship (Cano-Hila et al., 2017). This higher municipal investment is only partly motivated by the need to compensate for the reduction in available funds. Other, to some extent interconnected, goals include making BA less dependent on external resources and a project-based operating method that failed to guarantee sufficient stability and continuity of services, as well as enhancing active labour policy services, especially training, which had previously been neglected in favour of a strong emphasis on competitiveness and support for entrepreneurship as the main indirect way to generate employment. A further motive, as an interview with an expert on Barcelona's metropolitan strategic plans shows, relates to pressures stemming from BA workers' demand for more secure employment contracts.

This stability strengthened BA's role in the city economic and social context, making it a reference point and a kind of brand with a high reputation, both locally, as also emerged from interviews with young people who turned to BA for support to bring their business projects to fruition, and internationally (OECD, 2009). With 400 employees (Barcelona Activa, 2017), BA runs its main offices and a number of specialised facilities and comprehensive services related both to employment (professional advice, training, coaching) and to business support. Moreover, it is the main (pioneering) institution responsible for the promotion of entrepreneurship through high-tech/innovative start-up programmes and other services providing systematic, flexible, customised and accessible *soft* support[3] for aspiring entrepreneurs. This includes information sessions

[3] There are typically three types of entrepreneurial support: hard, soft and hybrid. The hard option involves financial aid. Soft assistance includes the provision of coaching/mentoring services and all actions conducive to the development of an entrepreneurial culture or mindset. Finally, hybrid forms of support employ both types of action (Sheehan & Namara, 2015).

delivered every week (welcome sessions) open to everyone and bookable online designed to present entrepreneurship support programmes and services as well as provide preliminary information regarding setting up a business in Barcelona (such as legal aspects and available funds). Even before the COVID-19 pandemic, remote welcome sessions were available, including in English, to attract entrepreneurs from abroad as well. After welcome sessions, initial appointments with entrepreneurship consultants are available to answer questions and respond to doubts about entrepreneurial projects and provide coaching services on business plans and fund-raising strategies. Support is offered throughout the year at the Glòries Entrepreneurship Centre (*Centro para la Iniciativa Emprendedora Glòries*) in district 22@ where aspiring entrepreneurs are given information, training classes and expert advice:

> from idea to business creation, what we do, at every step, is provide resources. On one hand, we give highly personalised advice. I can meet with a technician individually, explain my needs and the technician suggests the most appropriate training needs based on individual profile and needs. If the person involved is a tech entrepreneur who wants to get directly into an incubator, in this case there are services designed specifically for that business model and sector... we also offer several two-hour training sessions in which we also address very basic questions. If an entrepreneur doesn't have a clue, for example, there are sessions providing information on how to do a market study, how to price a product, how to identify a legal form, how to find funds, how to relate to people. (Entrepreneurship Directorate, BA, October 2017)

The approach adopted is "universal" in that any aspiring entrepreneur can apply for, and receive, information and/or support. In 2017, 14,395 people used its services and programmes, 7,441 people attended information sessions, 5,090 participated in business creation training and 2,126 entrepreneurial projects were supported (BA 2017).

Support for innovative start-ups comes from a network of incubators of which there were four in 2017.[4] These are specialised services designed to support the creation and growth of innovative companies by offering training and mentoring as well as support in attracting investors, offices

[4] New incubator projects were already emerging in 2017 and later led to the birth of two new (and different) incubators, as we will see in more detail in the next chapter of this book.

and other facilities. The Glòries Business Incubator was the first to be set up in 1986: "Barcelona Activa was set up solely to support entrepreneurs, 30 years ago it was founded as a business incubator" (Entrepreneurship Directorate, BA, October 2017). It is a 3,700 m^2 building with 60 workspaces measuring 18–110 m^2 to accommodate start-ups in their initial incubation period, a maximum of three years, in 2017. In addition to these workspaces, the centre has several video conferencing, meeting and training rooms as well as an auditorium and other recreational spaces (BA, 2017). In 2011, BA launched the Almogàvers Business Factory, a 4,872 m^2 incubator run by a public–private partnership based on a number of working relationships with universities, research centres, professional associations and financial institutions among others (BA, 2011). It provides support to high-tech start-ups and includes another coworking space. All this led to Barcelona being nominated European Capital of Innovation in 2014—the first—with one of the reasons being its promotion of strong alliances between research centres, universities and private and public partners.

The MediaTIC Incubator began work in 2017. It supports high-tech companies in areas such as artificial intelligence, the Internet of Things, big data and space technologies. Incubated enterprises benefit from various value-added services, including access to the physical space needed to develop their businesses, guidance, business advice and "ecosystem connections" (BA, 2017, p. 59). These three incubators are all located in district 22@. Another incubator is the Technology Business Centre for engineering-related technology companies. These initiatives reflect the city's efforts to accommodate socio-economic changes "continually progressing and demonstrating their quality and capacity to adapt to the needs of the market" (BA, 2016, p. 42). BA has, in fact, progressively modified and developed its services to meet changing aspiring entrepreneur "profiles" and "needs":

> today they have a more technological profile, so they no longer have the same needs they had 20 years ago. For example, the incubator was more designed to... it was not industrial, but it could provide lots of space, imagining large workforces... now a company that works, for example, with e-commerce, needs 15 to 20 square metres... so, we have been able to adapt our spaces and training and our team profiles as well. (Entrepreneurship Directorate, BA, October 2017)

The governance of these structures is based on a public–private partnership that is functional to the objective of working on "two levels", the former being the direct provision of services and the latter "the coordination of the city's entrepreneurial ecosystem". The aim is to "make the city attractive to foreign investors, for example" as well as to ensure a good city ranking: "I think we come fifth in the entrepreneurship rankings, that is, we are working very intensely on what allows us to position the city, to make it... let's say, friendly or attractive to entrepreneurs who are here or who want to come to Barcelona" (Entrepreneurship Directorate, BA, October 2017).

To this end, BA publishes annual activity reports and datasheets with eye-catching graphics showing the city's main economic indicators for marketing purposes emphasising characteristics of the city which enable it to be promoted as an ideal place to do business. Some of the most publicised of these are its geographical location, economic and specialisation diversification (e.g. ICT, tourism, commerce, congresses), universities, research and innovation centres, entrepreneurial dynamism and quality of life. For example, a report published in 2022 (also in English) closes with advertising messages targeting "companies", "entrepreneurs" and "professionals from all over the world" such as: "Do you want to expand your business in Barcelona? The Business Landing Service offers you a complete assistance when setting up your business in Barcelona". For entrepreneurs: "Do you want to set up your business in Barcelona? Barcelona Activa provides you with personalised plans that will guide you through while making your business activity in Barcelona a success and that will allow you to follow, step by step, the stages of setting up a business in Barcelona". While professionals are offered "a vibrant and welcoming city that makes it easy to land on a personal level and to connect with the local community thanks to the following resources: website with all the information you need to know if you move to the city; seminars, workshops, expat lunches, business visits around the city; welcome desk: online and face-to-face support for international talent" (Barcelona Activa, 2022).

Although support for entrepreneurship is just one component of Barcelona Activa's work—and placed third in terms of overall budgetary weight (11% in 2017, while 60% went to employment services)—it is a popular and important one. This stems from the role entrepreneurship plays in BA's long history and the importance of coordination and cooperation with the private sector, both of which have a decisive influence on BA's impact as well as its institutional publicity.

2.2.2 *Milan at the Local and National Dynamics Crossroads*

Growing prominence and material investment by Milan's local government in city policies supporting entrepreneurship began in 2011, as the new city administration took office. One of its underlying aims was to strengthen local government's leadership capacity in economic development processes, "to stimulate the city's growth", and contribute to giving the city:

> a leading role in the country's political and administrative innovation process, presenting Milan as a reference point internationally, too, with a leading position in many sectors - design, fashion, ITC new technologies - in value-added services and the creation of innovative enterprises. (Milan Municipality, 2016, p. 2)

Due consideration should be also paid to the role played by the central state. As Moisio and Rossi (2020) have shown, in Italy "the idea of start-up economies as engines of national innovation strategies gained currency during the post-recession years of the early 2010s, in times characterised by the harsh realities of fiscal austerity as well as by a spasmodic search for novel growth- and future-oriented rationales" (p. 538). These two scholars outlined the main national-level stages that brought the start-up economy concept to the centre of the political agenda. In particular, they highlighted the part played by the "technocratic" government set up in Italy in 2011 under the leadership of Mario Monti, a prominent economist at Milan's Bocconi University. In 2012 this government formally recognised innovative start-ups (in the Startup Act) on a special national register and both bureaucratic simplification measures and financial incentives (including "fast-track" and zero-cost incorporation and simplified insolvency procedures) were planned for their first 5 years. Support for start-ups continued under the subsequent government led by then-Democratic Party leader Matteo Renzi (2014–2016), with larger tax deductions and special funds set aside within the broader Industry 4.0 plan. The Renzi government's investment was also symbolic, with his first public visit being to a start-up incubator in Treviso in north-eastern

Italy and a trip to California in his first year, where he met the leaders of 150 Italian Silicon Valley start-ups, explaining that the government's commitment was to a "simpler country, with a different labour market,[5] with a slimmed down political class", and emphasising the importance of entrepreneurial ideas to socio-economic change.[6]

In this context, a number of both public and private sector initiatives have been set in motion in Milan since 2011 with a view to supporting entrepreneurship. According to data provided by the municipal report *Il Capitale Urbano* produced in 2021, the city has invested more than 45 million euros in Milan's "innovation ecosystem" since 2012 (City of Milan, 2021) through three main initiatives: grants to innovative start-ups in their early stages; active space and service networking, such as coworking, spinoffs, fablabs and makerspaces[7]; and support for innovation spaces and services such as accelerators and business incubators. The report also showcased Milan's achievements in the 2020 global innovation ecosystem report by Genome Startup (a private sector policy advisory and research organisation, one of the largest global start-up surveys) which ranked "Milan #30 out of the 100 emerging ecosystems that are gaining relevance and impacting the global startup scenario significantly" (City of Milan, 2021, p. 8), indicative of the symbolic value that these kinds of rankings now have in urban marketing and competition strategies (Pollio, 2020).

In particular, the municipality supported the setting up of the *Speed-MiUp* incubator in 2013 at Bocconi University, as part of the Employment and Entrepreneurship Support Agreement signed by the Chamber of Commerce and the City of Milan, with management of the incubator being entrusted to a consortium comprising the Chamber of Commerce and Bocconi University. Municipal support has also been forthcoming for other incubators, including PoliHub, which incubates about a hundred

[5] It is worth noting here that the government promoted a labour market reform (the Jobs Act) that sparked considerable opposition, especially to its limitations on workers' right to get their jobs back in the event of unfair dismissal.

[6] Renzi negli Usa incontra le startup italiane: "Serve cambiamento violento. Voi metteteci la forza delle vostre idee", *La Repubblica*, 22 Settembre 2014, available at: https://www.repubblica.it/politica/2014/09/22/news/renzi_in_silicon_valley_visita_twitter_e_yahoo-96386809/ (accessed 29 May 2023).

[7] A Fablab is a digital manufacturing laboratory. A makerspace is a hands-on learning venue which provides tools to "make things" and houses carpentry workshops, 3D printers, computing devices and manual tools for various uses, for example.

enterprises per year and is managed by Politecnico di Milano Foundation, and comprises public—including the municipality of Milan—and private sector entities such as Siemens, Pirelli and a2a. It was set up in 2013 on over 8,000 square metres of spaces in the former heavy industry city district of Bovisa with the additional aim of contributing to "giving this neighbourhood a new vitality" (Spaces Manager and Program Ambassador, PoliHub, April 2017). Another incubator supported was urban regeneration project Milano Luiss Hub, built on a total of 2,800 city centre square metres and managed by a public–private partnership (City of Milan, Luiss University, Brodolini Foundation, Italiacamp). It also supported BASE, a multi-function cultural centre occupying 12,000 square metres on three floors whose activities include the Teatro alla Scala laboratories-atelier, the Museum of Cultures-MUDEC and a space dedicated to cultural business incubation. It is run by a social enterprise made up of several social and cultural innovation companies and is located within the former Ansaldo complex, an early twentieth-century building purchased in the 1960s by Ansaldo to produce locomotives and railway and tram carriages. It was later dismantled before being bought up in the 1990s by the City of Milan and reconverted into a cultural centre.[8]

Finally, FabriQ is a socially innovative start-up incubator set up in 2014. It is the only such body owned by the municipality itself, although it is run by a temporary association of companies (the non-profit Brodolini Foundation and Impact Hub Milan, part of an international network of coworking-innovation labs). It is located in Quarto Oggiaro, a disadvantaged neighbourhood on the outskirts of Milan, and aims both to revitalise this neighbourhood and support social entrepreneurship including with a view to overcoming "the social sphere's voluntary legacy: people with social ideas do not automatically think of setting up in business, but rather of creating an association or something like that" (FabriQ Project Manager, January 2017). FabriQ offers hybrid support combining coaching services with economic incentives provided through municipal non-repayable grants (as expense reimbursements) via annual calls for proposals (2,051,000 EUR budgeted from 2014 to 2020; City of Milan, 2021). During my research period, covering the incubator's first three years, the projects selected by FabriQ's calls for proposals were given financial contributions of up to fifteen or twenty thousand euros

[8] Source: https://base.milano.it (accessed 29 May 2023).

depending on year, with which beneficiaries can cover up to 50% of the costs of setting up and/or running entrepreneurial project-related activities.

The municipal social innovation agenda has prioritised the creative production and sharing economy sectors, with an emphasis on makers (digital neo-manufacturing), fablabs, start-ups and coworking spaces (Pacchi, 2018), phenomena which favour a specific vision of social innovation[9] in which the market plays a particularly central role and which is often limited to specific social groups, such as young people with high levels of human capital directly involved in these emerging socio-economic sectors (Pasqui, 2018). Accordingly, approximately two-thirds of the thirty-two socially innovative start-ups supported in their first three years—on which my research focused—were digital economy sector firms, while others produced innovative devices or worked in knowledge-intensive business services. This incubator was also involved in entrepreneurship education programmes within local schools, with a view to promoting a youth entrepreneurship culture.

Support for innovative start-ups was primarily presented as a good way of dealing with the effects of the post-2008 economic crisis. As Torri (2017) documented, in 2011 the local government approved policy guidelines for employment policies and economic development which identified a series of key measures designed to foster entrepreneurship, technological and social innovation, the employment of the highly qualified and self-employment, with a particular emphasis on young people. Youth unemployment levels higher than those of the general population and "Neets"—i.e. young people not working, not studying and not in training—are the main focuses around which the problems underlying the implementation of entrepreneurship supports are defined. It should be noted, however, that problems tended to be given limited coverage during the interviews, with objectives, in particular, being a preferred topic. As one interview clearly emphasised: "we try not to reason in terms of problems, or gaps to be bridged, but to start from potential in order to

[9] In scholarly debate the concept of social innovation may refer to the way in which state, market and civil society relations are being redefined in the context of the welfare state crisis. Following the political rise of a concept which has been central to the EU's policy agenda since 2010 several critics highlighted its affinity with neoliberal thinking and the progressive centrality it accords the market and models of neoliberal subjectivities (e.g. Fougère et al., 2017). For a discussion of the concept and Milan's social innovation agenda, see Bifulco and Dodaro (2019).

expand it" (Urban Economy and Employment Directorate, Milan Municipality, February 2017). The city's "vocation" or "roots", as exemplified in a distinctive entrepreneurial ethos, are referenced in particular as the main source of the municipal strategy's legitimacy:

> It might be said that the roots of this work lie in Milan's city fabric, its specific context. Evidently, Milan is the economic and financial centre of the country, one of the most significant places from this point of view, hence the political mandate to try to use these assets to lever a triggering, multiplier effect. It is a matter of using public policies to enhance excellence, an extremely fertile and lively fabric. (Economic Planning Unit, Milan Municipality, April 2017)

As an official of the Urban Economy and Labour Department put it, "this local government has tried to shine the spotlight on, and reinforce, a pre-existing emphasis of the city of Milan's" (March 2017). However, definitions and non-definitions of the problems underlying policy initiatives in general are not neutral, as the coherence between this approach to the local political culture, on the one hand, and the central role of private economic initiative in Milanese governance and MESPs, on the other, highlights. A novel aspect deserving of attention is the greater visibility accorded new economic actors, "making another Milan, another city, visible" (ivi), in reference to third sector organisations, social innovators, makerspaces and coworking, often associated to the segment—mainly young and often highly educated—of the urban population whose response to labour market challenges is self-employment and entrepreneurship bound up with emerging economic opportunities (Pacchi, 2018).

2.3 Radicalising Urban Entrepreneurialism?

The rise of the start-up economy has had a tangible impact on cities. As Moisio and Rossi (2020) also noted, international organisations, nation states, transnational networks of cities and, at the local level, strong partnerships between strategic actors—including universities, research centres, chambers of commerce, foundations and private sector companies among others—seem to be converging around the goal of actively promoting the city as the ideal place for innovative and technological start-ups. Competition takes the form of rankings and classifications, and Milan and

Barcelona are vying for primacy as hubs of innovation and entrepreneurship: "Barcelona's entrepreneurial ecosystem is growing and the city is reinforcing itself as one of the best places to launch a start-up in Europe" (Barcelona Activa, 2017, p. 61). The frequency with which these latter words recur is noteworthy. "The best place to launch a start-up" is the slogan of Milanese incubator Speed MI Up but it is a phrase which stands out in the websites and discourses of cities the world over. City areas renewed and reconverted for this purpose provide further examples of both material and symbolic investment whose purpose is to strengthen visibility and consolidate cities as entrepreneurial ecosystems, understood as networks of actors and sets of infrastructures, services, programmes and, in general, a favourable climate for entrepreneurship. Success in this venture has both symbolic and material foundations. The former are bound up with persuasive capacity facilitated by a "positive hegemonic discourse on entrepreneurship" (Essers et al., 2017, p. 5) mobilising Schumpeterian accounts of entrepreneurship seen as key to the innovation, change, attractiveness and competitiveness of economic systems, interlocking with that other powerful imaginary, the knowledge economy (Jessop & Sum, 2010). Persuasive capacity also potentially relies on the vague, prescriptive, decontextualised and depoliticised narrative that entrepreneurship in general is suffused with (see Chapter 1). The very concept of start-up, now common parlance, is rather elusive. While it is generally employed to refer to innovative enterprises, it is also sometimes used simply to indicate entrepreneurial organisation's nascent stage. Moreover, as Luise (2019) pointed out, innovation can mean many things and even a "pizzeria with a website" can be listed on the Italian Chamber of Commerce's register of innovative start-ups (p. 19). The next chapter further elaborates on this point.

Finally, innovative entrepreneurship's popularity is influenced by multilevel dynamics, resulting from the leading promotional role played by both important political bodies such as the European Union, on the one hand, and nation states, on the other. In this respect, the institutional support provided by international bodies and states in this field is "impressive", as Fiorentino (2018) argued, and I would, to some extent, agree that it "has to be read as a top-down strategy to rebrand and relocate city economies towards new sectors" (p. 117), i.e. technological, digital and knowledge-based sectors. However, this chapter shows the variegated form taken by convergence dynamics in the two cities, and highlights their different time frames, modalities, governance models and features, influenced by their specific historical and institutional legacies, culture and local socio-economic characteristics. It also shows the very active role cities play in this. This may reflect the way in which "the late neoliberal city has ingested and internalised the entrepreneurial logics itself", to put it in Peck's words (2014, p. 399). However, this makes exploring how entrepreneurship-related discourses and strategies can be recontextualised by local actors and potentially reoriented towards multiple purposes of even greater interest.

References

Aldrich, H. E., Ruef, M. (2018). Unicorns, gazelles, and other distractions on the way to understanding real entrepreneurship in the United States. *Academy of Management Perspectives*, *32*(4), 458–472.

Andreotti, A., & Le Galès, P. (2019). Introduzione. In *Governare Milano nel nuovo millennio* (pp. 7–41). il Mulino.

Armondi, S., Di Vita, S. (2018). *Milan. Productions, Spatial Patterns and Urban Change*. Routledge.

Arvidsson, A., & Luise, V. (2019). Il sistema delle startup e l'innovazione possible. *il Mulino* (6), 973–980.

Assolombarda. (2021). *Booklet. Italy, Lombardy and Milan*. Assolombarda.

Barcelona Activa. (2011). *Memoria de actividades*. Barcelona Activa.

Barcelona Activa. (2016). *Activity report 2016*. Barcelona Activa.

Barcelona Activa. (2017). *Activities report 2017*. Barcelona Activa.

Barcelona Activa. (2020). *Barcelona. Datasheet 2020*. Barcelona Activa.

Barcelona Activa. (2022). *Barcelona. Main economic indicators for the Barcelona area*. Barcelona Activa.

Benassi, D. (2019). Il governo del sistema di assistenza sociale in una prospettiva di lungo period. In A. Andreotti (Ed.), *Governare Milano nel nuovo millennio* (pp. 71–95). il Mulino.

Bifulco, L., & Dodaro, M. (2019). Local welfare governance and social innovation: The ambivalence of the political dimension. In *Politics and conflict in governance and planning. Theory and practice* (pp. 169–185). Routledge.

Blakeley, G. (2005). Local governance and local democracy: The Barcelona model. *Local Government Studies*, *31*(2), 149–165.

Blakeley, G. (2010). Governing ourselves: Citizen participation and governance in Barcelona and Manchester. *International Journal of Urban and Regional Research*, *34*(1), 130–145.

Brenner, N. (2004). Urban governance and the production of new state spaces in western Europe, 1960–2000. *Review of International Political Economy, 11*(3), 447–488.
Cano-Hila, A., Pradel, M., & Garcia, M. (2017). Barcelona. Policies for social cohesion in the context of urban competitiveness. In R. Cucca, & C. Ranci (Eds.), *Unequal cities: The challenge of post-industrial transition in times of austerity*. Routledge.
Charnock, G., Purcell, T. F., & Ribera-Fumaz, R. (2013). City of rents: The limits to the Barcelona model of urban competitiveness. *International Journal of Urban and Regional Research, 38*(1), 198–217.
Charnock, G., & Ribera-Fumaz, R. (2023). El distrito 22@Barcelona: ¿Una "plataforma de innovación" urbana o la urbanización del capitalismo de plataformas? *EMPIRIA. Revista de Metodología de Ciencias Sociales* (59), 159–187.
Chiarello, F. (2017). Presentazione. *Quaderni di Sociologia, 73*, 3–7.
City of Milan. (2021). *Il capitale urbano.* Comune di Milano.
Costa, G., Cucca, R., & Torri, S. (2016). Milan: A city lost in the transition from the growth machine paradigm towards a social innovation approach. In T. Brandsen, S. Cottacin, A. Evers, & A. Zimmer (Eds.), *Social innovation in the urban context* (pp. 125–142). Springer.
Cottacin, S., & Zimmerman, A. (2016). Urban governance and social innovations. In T. Brandsen, S. Cottacin, A. Evers, & A. Zimmer (Eds.), *Social innovation in the urban context* (pp. 21–44). Springer.
Crossa, V., Pareja-Eastaway, M., & Barber, A. (2010). Reinventing the city: Barcelona, Birmingham and Dublin. In S. Musterd & A. Murie (Eds.), *Making competitive cities* (pp. 67–92). Wiley-Blackwell.
Cucca, R., & Maestripieri, L. (2017). Varieties of post-Fordist transitions and labour market inequalities. In R. Cucca & C. Ranci (Eds.), *Unequal cities: The challenge of post-industrial transition in times of austerity* (pp. 21–44). Routledge.
Cucca, R., & Ranci, C. (2017). *Unequal cities: The challenge of post-industrial transition in times of austerity*. Routledge.
Degen, M., & García, M. (2012). The transformation of the "Barcelona model": An analysis of culture, urban regeneration and governance. *International Journal of Urban and Regional Research, 36*(5), 1022–1038.
D'Ovidio, M. (2016). *The creative city does not exist. Critical essays on the creative and cultural economy of cities*. Ledizioni.
Essers, C., Dey, P., Tedmanson, D., & Verduyn, K. (2017). *Critical perspectives on entrepreneurship. Challenging dominant discourses*. Routledge.
Eurocities. (2013). *Cities supporting inclusive entrepreneurship.* Eurocities.

Fiorentino, S. (2018). Re-making urban economic geography. Start-ups, entrepreneurial support and the makers movement: A critical assessment of policy mobility in Rome. *Geoforum, 93*, 116–119.

Florida, R. (2002). *The rise of the creative class*. Basic Books.

Fougère, M., Segercrantz, B., & Seeck, H. (2017). A critical reading of the European Union's social innovation policy discourse: (Re)legitimizing neoliberalism. *Organization, 1*(25), 1–25.

García, M. (1993). Local economic policies and social citizenship in Spanish cities. *Antipode, 25*(3), 191–205.

García, M., & Judd, D. (2012). Competitive cities. In K. Mossberger, P. John, & S. Clark (Eds.), *The (Oxford) handbook of urban politics* (pp. 486–500). Oxford University Press.

Gentile, A. (2011). Urban governance of employment activation. The case of Barcelona Activa (Spain). *Urbe. Revista Brasileira de Gestão Urbana, 3*, 41–54.

Guerrini, F. (2017). From self-made entrepreneurs to the sharing economy: Milan as a laboratory for a new collaboration-based approach. In P. Formica (Ed.), *Entrepreneurial renaissance. Cities striving towards an era of rebirth and revival* (pp. 89–99). Springer.

Harvey, D. (1989). From managerialism to entrepreneurialism: The transformation in urban governance in late capitalism. *Geografiska Annaler. Series B, Human Geography, 71*(1), 3–17.

Jessop, B. (2004). Critical semiotic analysis and cultural political economy. *Critical Discourse Studies, 1*(2), 159–174.

Jessop, B. (2010). Cultural political economy and critical policy studies. *Critical Policy Studies, 3*(3–4), 336–356.

Jessop, B., & Oosterlynck, S. (2008). Cultural political economy: On making the cultural turn without falling into soft economic sociology. *Geoforum, 39*(3), 1155–1169.

Jessop, B., & Sum, N. L. (2010). Cultural political economy: Logics of discovery, epistemic fallacies, the complexity of emergence, and the potential of the cultural turn. *New Political Economy, 15*(3), 445–451.

Langley, P., & Leyshon, A. (2016). Platform capitalism: The intermediation and capitalisation of digital economic circulation. *Finance and Society, 2*(1), 1–21.

Luise, V. (2019). *Le forme dell'innovazione nell'ideologia californiana: Le retoriche, i modelli e le trasformazioni nell'economia startup*. Egea.

Milan Chamber of Commerce. (2015). *Milano Produttiva 2015*. Pearson Italia.

Milan Municipality. (2016). *Report delle attività e degli interventi realizzati dal 2012 al 2016*. Comune di Milano.

Mingione, E., dell'Agnese, E., Mugnano, S., d'Ovidio, M., Niessen, B., & Sedini, C. (2007). *Milan city-region: Is it still competitive and charming? Pathways to creative and knowledge-based regions*. AMIDSt, University of Amsterdam.

Moisio, S., & Rossi, U. (2020). The start-up state: Governing urbanised capitalism. *EPA: Economy and Space, 52*(3), 532–552.

Mugnano, S., Murphy, E., Martin-Brelot, H. (2010). Strategic Economic Policy: Milan, Dublin and Toulouse. *In Making Competitive Cities, edited by A. Musterd and S. Murie*, 244–262. Oxford: Wiley-Blackwell.

OECD. (2009). *Promoting entrepreneurship, employment and business competitiveness: The experience of Barcelona*. OECD.

Pacchi, C. (2018). Sharing economy. Makerspaces, co-working spaces, hybrid workplaces, and new social practices. In S. Armondi & S. Di Vita (Eds.), *Milan. Productions, spatial patterns and urban change* (pp. 73–83). Routledge.

Pareja-Eastaway, M., & Pradel, M. (2015). Towards the creative and knowledge economies: Analysing diverse pathways in Spanish cities towards the creative and knowledge economies: Analysing diverse pathways in Spanish cities. *European Planning Studies, 23*(12), 2404–2422.

Pasqui, G. (2018). The last cycle of Milan urban policies and the prospects for a new urban agenda. In S. Armondi & S. Di Vita (Eds.), *Milan. Productions, spatial patterns and urban change* (pp. 133–144). Routledge.

Peck, J. (2014). Entrepreneurial urbanism: Between uncommon sense and dull compulsion. *Geografiska Annaler, Series B: Human Geography, 96*(4), 396–401.

Pollio, A. (2020). Making the silicon cape of Africa: Tales, theories and the narration of startup urbanism. *Urban Studies, 57*(13), 2715–2732.

Pradel, M., Cano-Hila, A. B., & García, M. (2020). *Urban governance and social innovation. Citizenship, civil society and social movements*. Edward Elgar.

Rosa, G. (2009). *Il mito della capitale morale*. Edizioni di comunità.

Rossi, U. (2017). *Cities in global capitalism*. Polity Press.

Rossi, U., & Di Bella, A. (2017). Start-up urbanism: New York, Rio de Janeiro and the global urbanization of technology-based economies. *Environment and Planning A, 49*(5), 999–1018.

Rossi, U., & Vanolo, Z. (2010). *Geografia politica urbana*. Laterza.

Sassen, S. (2007). *A sociology of globalization*. W. W. Norton.

Sheehan, M., Namara, A.M. (2015) Business Start-Ups and Youth Self-Employment *A Policy Literature Review Synthesis Report*, STYLE Working Papers, WP7.1. CROME. University of Brighton

Sternberg, C. (2023). *Neoliberal urban governance. Spaces, culture and discourses in Buenos Aires and Chicago*. Palgrave Macmillan.

Torri, R. (2017). Milan. Challenging the private interest government in times of austerity. In *Unequal cities: The challenge of post-industrial transition in times of austerity*. Routledge.
Trullén, J. (2002). Barcelona como ciudad flexible. Economías de localización y economías de urbanización en una metrópolis polinuclear. In G. Becattini, M. T. Costa, & J. Trullén (Eds.), *Desarrollo local: teorías y estrategias* (pp. 204–275). Editorial Civitas.

CHAPTER 3

Inclusive Entrepreneurship Policies: Reproducing Heterogeneity, Negotiating Ambivalence

Abstract This chapter critically discusses the Schumpeterian view of entrepreneurship prevalent in the start-up city rhetoric, taking a closer look at entrepreneurship programme implementation and outcomes in Barcelona and Milan and the emergence of "inclusive" approaches to entrepreneurship support policies. Furthermore, it will attempt to shine the spotlight on the heterogeneity underlying entrepreneurship and consider how this is replicated through policies on various levels in contexts of deeper individualisation. It highlights the relevance of the principles of activation and responsibilisation that has generally informed social policies in recent decades in EU states' and city entrepreneurship policies as well, and the way this contributes to generating opaque definitions of entrepreneurship with ambivalent outcomes. At the same time, it will also illustrate the way local policy actors negotiate views of entrepreneurship and its ambivalence, in an attempt to exert control over the goals and outcomes of their work.

Keywords Inclusive entrepreneurship · Entrepreneurship ambivalence · Individualisation · Barcelona · Milan · Start-up city · Local actors agency

> Cities - and for that matter other spatial formations - are not purposeful or bounded economic entities, but sites where the full variety of the 'economy

M. Dodaro, *Unpacking the 'Start-up City'*,
https://doi.org/10.1007/978-3-031-50212-5_3

> in general' is made visible and juxtaposed, but with crucial effects resulting from the particularities of 'placement'. The urban is not just a microcosm of the world, a window through which the economy can be read, but also a forcing house with considerable power to drive and shape the economy through its gatherings.
>
> (Amin & Thrift, 2007, p. 150)

The city as a microcosm and force field—the latter in Bourdieu's words—is the twofold status that the above two geographers attribute to the city and the urban economy. By "microcosm" they mean the city's ability to condense global dynamics into spatially bounded spaces while the term "force field" points to a plural, incoherent and conflicting domain of practices and logics which cannot be reduced to a single homogeneous whole. This chapter and those which follow will strive to maintain a focus on both dimensions, and take a close look at the "everyday city". This latter term is used by Amin and Thrift in reference to the ordinary life facet of the urban world which takes shape from each city's specific economic, labour market and housing conditions, local welfare system, spatial and built environment and formal and informal relationships and exchanges. It is a shadowy facet of city life which the two scholars describe as "the other" or "old" urban, sometimes labelled "worthless" and often "deemed to be dull" and "despite its continuing relevance for large chunks of urban economic life, to be choked off" (2007, p. 152). Similarly, entrepreneurship which might be described as everyday, old, traditional or ordinary is often overshadowed by Californian ideology and the Schumpeterian view of urban entrepreneurship and municipal entrepreneurship support policies (MESPs).

This chapter will attempt to shine the spotlight on the heterogeneity underlying entrepreneurship and consider how this is replicated through policies on various levels in contexts of deeper individualisation. It highlights the relevance of the principles of activation and responsibilisation that have generally informed social policies in recent decades in EU states' and city entrepreneurship policies as well, and the way this contributes to generating opaque definitions of entrepreneurship with ambivalent outcomes. At the same time, it will also illustrate the way local policy actors negotiate views of entrepreneurship and its ambivalence, in an attempt to exert control over the goals and outcomes of their work.

3.1 Entrepreneurship: A Contested Concept

No study dealing with entrepreneurship can sidestep the entrepreneur and entrepreneurship definition issue. The term entrepreneur dates back to the sixteenth century, when it designated a captain of fortune responsible for recruiting mercenary troops for princes or cities, but it was not until the second half of the eighteenth century that the first theoretical interpretations of the concept were attempted, starting with economist Cantillon, who saw entrepreneurship as consisting of taking on the risks involved in organising production and the activities inherent in it (Gallino, 1978). Classical sociologists such as Sombart, Simmel and Weber examined the issue in the context of their studies on the origins of capitalism, but it is Schumpeter's first half of the twentieth-century theories that are central to theoretical reflection on entrepreneurship. These theories notoriously fuse entrepreneurship with innovation (understood as the introduction of new goods, production methods, raw materials and forms of organisation and the opening up of new markets) implying a number of limitations for sociological research. For instance, by this definition "many past and present entrepreneurs - identifiable and tangible subjects for research - are not entrepreneurs at all [...] as they act in a routine or traditional way". A further limitation arises "because the only discriminating factor in this entrepreneur definition is the moment an innovation is brought in. Schumpeterian man may well own a business for his entire life, with all the power and interests that come with this, but be an entrepreneur only for one day" (Gallino, 1978, p. 370, author's translation).

Overall, difficulties in delimiting the entrepreneurship concept, both theoretically and empirically, are a constant in the social sciences. Reasons for this relate to a lack of systematic theorisations, but also to a long-standing marginalisation of the subject even in the economic literature (Arum & Müller, 2004; Swedberg, 2000). In this respect, note that forms of entrepreneurship such as small businesses and self-employment have long appeared likely to be squeezed out by large-scale Fordist corporations. It is only since the 1980s that this latter fear began to dissipate following on from a reappraisal of the importance of both industrial districts in economic development and economic tertiarisation processes (Arum & Müller, 2004; Fellini, 2010). A further reason lies in the inherently ever-changing and contingent character of entrepreneurship, which is always closely bound up with its economic and socio-institutional context (Pirone, 2023). Thus attempts to distinguish "genuine", i.e. more or less innovative entrepreneurs, from those who run businesses in general do not always succeed in reducing the ambiguities of existing definitions. This is especially true in the context of the socio-institutional changes at work in contemporary capitalism, which is described as "entrepreneurial" (Marchesnay, 2012) to the extent that it celebrates the autonomy, independence, creativity, excellence and personal self-fulfilment typically associated with entrepreneurial rationality as core values.

In actual fact, the rise of entrepreneurship is also inextricably bound up with the rise of neoliberalism and what Foucault (2005) called "neoliberal governmentality", namely a set of devices designed to encourage the behaviour by which individuals become enterprises. These self-entrepreneurs compete, invent and reinvent themselves, take a corporate approach to their lives and are their own masters.

In such a contest any definition is blurred and ambivalent. As a young nascent entrepreneur told me in an interview: "I think you can be an entrepreneur in many ways. It's not just setting up a business. For me, entrepreneurship can also be learning new things, signing up for courses, it doesn't have to be necessarily starting a business (...) *emprender* something [in Spanish] means starting something. In the sense of starting something new" (Letitia, 29, handicraft production and sale, Barcelona, February 2018).

Social scientists tend to converge on broad conceptualisations which typically define entrepreneurs as business owners, and entrepreneurship as the process of creating new business organisations, an approach endorsed by the Global Entrepreneurship Monitor (GEM) scholarship team, among others, and adopted in its global annual monitoring research since 1997. More precisely, GEM scholars define entrepreneurship as "any attempt at new business or new venture creation, such as self-employment, a new business organization, or the expansion of an existing business, by an individual, a team of individuals, or an established business".[1] This definition seeks to take into account the uncertainty that generally characterises the nascent entrepreneurship phases[2] and

[1] "How Gem defines Entrepreneurship", available at: https://www.gemconsortium.org/wiki/1149 (accessed 13 June 2023).

[2] "The Nascent Entrepreneur has actively devoted resources to starting the business but the business has not yet paid wages or salaries (including to themselves) for a period of three months" (GEM, 2023, p. 30).

to encompass both informal (unregulated) and formal entrepreneurship (GEM, 2023). There is no single definition of entrepreneurship even in everyday parlance and still less in public policy. The sections which follow outline the way entrepreneurship are increasingly seen as a heterogeneous field in the European normative context. The European Union is indeed one of the most influential institutions promoting policy ideas, principles and strategies for both member states and cities (Scalise, 2020).

3.2 Inclusive Entrepreneurship

The promotion of entrepreneurship, in many cases flanked by self-employment, has long been high on the European agenda. In particular, it feeds into both economic development and employment policies, and active labour market policies. Employment policies entail measures designed to increase total employment, while labour market policies target specific categories of the labour force identified on the basis of the labour market difficulties they face, such as the unemployed, young people, women and migrants (Lodigiani & Scippa, 2014). Deciding which of the two policy domains entrepreneurship support measures fall into is no easy task, since such measures are typically employed with a view to simultaneously fostering the creation of businesses with a potential to hire workers—thus increasing employment rates—and enhancing self-employment in specific categories of workers. This dual approach has consolidated entrepreneurship as a key European Employment Strategy (EES) policy. The EES was launched in 1997 with a view to providing guidelines and coordinating labour market and social policy reforms across member countries, focusing on four main dimensions: employability, adaptability, equal opportunities and entrepreneurship. Attention to self-employment and entrepreneurship in European strategies has remained unwavering since (Lodigiani & Scippa, 2014) as a great many initiatives confirm, including the Entrepreneurship 2020 Action Plan adopted in January 2013. The plan recommends action to foster entrepreneurship such as removing key barriers and nurturing a culture of entrepreneurship to ensure "that being an entrepreneur is an attractive prospect for Europeans" (European Commission, 2013, p. 5). The plan pays particular attention to three aspects: fostering entrepreneurship education among young people; increasing entrepreneurial opportunities for under-represented groups, with a special focus on women; and creating an environment conducive to business creation, e.g. simplifying administrative requirements and improving attractiveness to investors. In 2017 the European Commission also introduced measures designed to support entrepreneurship in its industrial policy strategy, outlined in the document *Investing in smart, innovative and sustainable industry—A renewed EU industrial policy strategy* which focuses on automation and digitalisation and innovative sectors such as robotics, the internet of things, artificial intelligence, energy systems and the bio-economy.

This innovation focus is always flanked by a marked emphasis on inclusive entrepreneurship, in line with the Europe 2020 Strategy goal of supporting inclusive growth. In this regard, the European Commission has been working with the OECD to encourage an inclusive approach to entrepreneurship policies, which both bodies consider to contribute to reducing inequality, for more than a decade. This collaboration has sparked several initiatives, including the Better Entrepreneurship Policy Tool,[3] policy briefs, country-specific policy analyses, best practice compendia and, since 2013, the *Missing Entrepreneurs* book series. Their main purpose is outlined in the following extract:

> Inclusive entrepreneurship policies seek to ensure that all people have an opportunity to be successful as an entrepreneur. This includes policies and programmes that help people from groups that are under-represented and disadvantaged in the labour market (i.e. women, youth, seniors, the unemployed, immigrants and people with disabilities) in starting and growing businesses. The objective is to move more people into work via self-employment to allow people an opportunity to participate economically and socially, and to generate income for themselves. (OECD/European Commission, 2017, p. 15)

The reference benchmark is entrepreneurship rates for men in the 30–49 age bracket, which would, the latest report states, lead to 9 million additional people starting and running new businesses in the European Union if it were to be matched by other groups (OECD/European

[3] The Better Entrepreneurship Policy Tool targets public and private sector stakeholders involved in designing and/or implementing entrepreneurship programmes (national and local policymakers, chambers of commerce, business associations, universities and research institutions, NGOs, etc.). This is an online tool offering a self-assessment questionnaire on inclusive and social entrepreneurship programmes in a given region or country and providing policy guidelines and best practices to inspire policy and programme design, https://betterentrepreneurship.eu/en/content/about-better-entrepreneurship-tool (accessed: 13 June 2023).

Commission, 2021, p. 21). Barriers to be broken down via targeted policies include limited access to finance, skill shortages and low social capital, as well as others related to the socio-institutional context such as lack of care services and poor entrepreneurial culture. The underlying argument is that, in many cases, start-up incentives prove "more effective and efficient in reducing unemployment than other active labour market policies, particularly for the low-skilled" (European Commission, 2014, p. 5).

On a normative level, the activation paradigm provides a political and institutional framework for inclusive policies supporting entrepreneurship. Entrepreneurship, in turn, embodies its underlying philosophy and conception of citizenship founded on employment as the main lever of social inclusion and well-being, and autonomous, active and responsible individuals (Lodigiani & Scippa, 2014). Priority in the activation principle, in fact, is accorded to active or "activable" population entry into the labour market, for example, those not formally employed and not looking for work. The importance of this principle lies in the fact that it constitutes a real paradigm shift from welfare-state-based notions, from the logic of protection against social risks (e.g. unemployment or illness) to individual responsibilisation and autonomy (Bifulco, 2017; Borghi, 2011; van Berkel & Møller, 2002), albeit its translation at the local level is rather different from one context to another (Scalise, 2020).

Support programmes for entrepreneurship have also expanded in Italy and Spain, particularly in the wake of the 2008 crisis, with a particular emphasis on young people. In Spain, a key move in this direction was the national youth employment plans (Entrepreneurship and Youth Employment Strategy 2013–2016 and Youth Employment Plan 2019–2021) and the Youth Guarantee Initiative (OECD/European Commission, 2017, 2019, 2021; Scalise, 2020) which performed a similar function in Italy. National level programmes are matched by local initiatives with the latter being the sphere in which primary responsibility for the formulation of active labour policies lies in both countries. Furthermore, in line with the framework outlined above, not only have several major European cities undertaken a range of initiatives to support entrepreneurship, as discussed below, but they have also implemented inclusive policies and programmes as well (Eurocities, 2013).

As far as city governance and policy are concerned, Pill (2021, p. 110) has recently underlined that support for local firms and start-up stimulation on an inclusive basis can potentially be interpreted in multiple ways. For some it shifts the focus from growth and competition for investment and human capital to supporting local economic and labour market entry and self-entrepreneurship initiatives from specific social groups and locally rooted institutions (such as universities) (see Torri, 2017). Others see such initiatives as mixing up cause and effect by attempting to reduce inequality through market mechanisms in line with a neoliberal (pro-market) urban governance approach, itself the source of inequality. The following sections show a more complex picture by exploring the inclusive entrepreneurship initiatives implemented in Barcelona and Milan and enquiring into social actor agency, building on a focus on the ways in which structured entrepreneurship heterogeneity intersects with, and is generated by, equally variegated policy instruments.

3.3 Diversified Policy Instruments in Diversified Urban Economies

Chapter 2 of this volume sketched out the complexity and diversity characterising the urban economies of Barcelona and Milan set against the backdrop of an expanding tertiary sector. Theories such as the creative city and "entrepreneurial city" urban marketing strategies have contributed to shining the spotlight on advanced services, urban middle class professionalisation processes (managers, architects, fashion designers and other skilled professions) and in general phenomena most consistent with the innovative, creative, attractive city image, while masking its contradictions and weaknesses (D'Ovidio, 2016). We have also seen that service expansion has not only implied an increase in jobs for the highly educated and qualified, but also in sectors such as catering, retail and the gig economy characterised by low wages, poor working conditions and greater job instability and insecurity (Eurofond, 2017; Sassen, 2006).

It should also be noted that the tertiarisation of the economy has also had a significant impact on self-employment and entrepreneurship which has grown in both advanced and non-advanced services, the sectors in which most self-employment is concentrated (Eurofond, 2017). The expansion of the service sector, as opposed to capital-intensive industry, has reduced costs and increased opportunities for self-employment (Arum & Müller, 2004). Even the COVID-19 pandemic left this unchanged, although its effect on a significant entrepreneurship segment was serious. In fact, the temporary closure of some business sectors inevitably discouraged new business creation and jeopardised existing ones. Eurostat data shows that in 2020, three quarters (66%) of all active EU enterprises were working in the service sector, employing approximately two-thirds of the total employed population (Eurostat, 2022a). Once again in 2020, almost a quarter (24.3%) of the EU's 23.4 million non-financial businesses were classified as commerce (motor vehicle, wholesale and retail trade), while almost one in five (19.2%) were classified as professional, scientific and technical. Furthermore, more than nine out of ten (93.5%) EU firms were low added value micro-enterprises (fewer than 10 employees) (Eurostat, 2022b).

In this context, both Milan and Barcelona have a relatively high number of active enterprises. Eurostat data shows that there were more than three hundred thousand of these in the province of Milan and five hundred thousand in Barcelona in 2019. Of these, the majority are zero employee companies (61% in Barcelona and 67% in Milan), followed by those with 1–9 employees (34% in Barcelona and 27% in Milan), with the rest made up of firms with workforces of over 10.[4] Local chamber of commerce data for 2019 shows that most of Milan's active enterprises are service sector firms (51.1%) and, more specifically within this, real estate (9.9%), professional, scientific and technical (9%), accommodation and food (6.5%), business support (5.6%) and other services. Next in importance, with 24.2% of active enterprises, were wholesale and retail trade, followed by construction (13.5%) and manufacturing (9.4%) (Milan Chamber of Commerce, 2020). In the same year, Barcelona's active enterprises were primarily in the business services sector (27.5%), which includes professional, scientific, technical and administrative services, followed by commerce (17.2%), education, health and social services (10.2%), real estate (8.2%), construction (8.1%), hospitality (6.1%) and other services (5.1%) (Barcelona Activa, 2020).

Like other southern European cities, Milan and Barcelona are thus small business and professional cities, meaning that both economic systems are characterised by a considerably entrepreneurial culture, with a significant share of sole traders. Within this framework local governments face multiple pressures and not only from the top down. The promotion of entrepreneurship (and self-employment) also stems from bottom-up drives. Self-employment culture and the social and cultural embeddedness of entrepreneurship are elements which contribute to

[4] Data source: Eurostat, Business demography by size, class and NUTS 3 regions (online data code: BD_SIZE_R3) retrieved from: https://ec.europa.eu/eurostat/web/regions/data/database (accessed: 01 July 2023).

constructing the composite framework within which entrepreneurship support programmes in Milan and Barcelona take shape. The following sections illustrate how action supporting innovative start-ups is flanked by attempts to shore up what we will henceforth call *ordinary* entrepreneurship, to distinguish it from the innovative variety. This term is designed to shine the spotlight on entrepreneurship located somewhere in the middle of the Schumpeterian variant and a more opaque one, sometimes located beyond the legality frontier. Indeed, one of the forms taken by labour de-regulation and precarisation is the rise of the so-called economically dependent or false self-employed, characterised by greater short- and long-term financial vulnerability, a number of gaps in social protection and generally poor working conditions (Borghi & Murgia, 2019; Eurofond, 2017). The concept of *ordinariness* was initially employed to explore the experiences of younger beneficiaries, drawing on sociological studies on youth, in which several scholars distinguish "ordinary youth" from the "more excluded or more spectacular youth" (Woodman, 2013, p. 179). I have employed it to distinguish also between innovative enterprises and other kinds of business.

3.3.1 Embracing Heterogeneity: The Case of Barcelona

Barcelona Activa, as we have already seen, has adopted an intervention model that provides, firstly, a base of soft support accessible to all. It also offers specialised and dedicated services to innovative enterprises mainly through its network of incubators and a range of programmes aimed at specific target groups or economic sectors on a regular basis. In particular, there are entrepreneurship support programmes for young people aged 16–30 with business ideas in any economic sector, such as the *Ideas amb Futur* Programme. Other programmes target adults over the age of 45 (*Ideas Maduras*) or women (*Inicia* programme). Alongside these programmes, there are sector-specific ones encouraging enterprise creation, for example, in the social and solidarity economy (hereafter SSE), social entrepreneurship, craft production, creative industry and trade fields. Albeit with some variations from year to year, these are run periodically, and applied for online when registration opens. For example, 684 participants registered on tailor-made business creation programmes and 284 on sector programmes in 2019 (BA, 2019).

Most of these take place at the Civic Centre Sant Agustí Convent, and whose purpose is "informing, orienting, motivating, educating and promoting employment and entrepreneurship in Barcelona", with a focus on social inclusion. The Convent dates back to the fourteenth century and is located in Ciutat Vella, the city's historical centre, thus is spatially separate from the BA headquarters and the 22@ district:

> Here we work a little differently, methodologically speaking. There [at the Glòries centre] people can follow an itinerary with training capsules, sign up, then come back and sign up for another one... when they need specific advice or have doubts they ask for the Glòries technical team's consultancy service... here we have programmes that are for 20 or 25 people who are the same throughout the programme, and then we deliver what we might call the basic training needed by business start-ups. Most programme hours deal with the development of business plans, a fundamental tool. (Consultant, St Augusti Convent, January 2018)

These programmes target specific groups (e.g. young people, women or the over-50s) regardless of business project type (technological, socially innovative, commercial, etc.). However, these mostly cover ordinary entrepreneurial initiatives, i.e. in traditional, mostly trade sectors. Such programmes, therefore, strengthen support for a large and diverse segment of BA's target population, despite most of the entrepreneurs it helps being university graduates (these accounted for 72% in 2018, for example; see BA, 2019). In particular, out of a total of 13,780 service- and programme-users in 2018, of which 2,371 were projects supported by a technical team and/or through dedicated programmes, 210 were innovative businesses or projects set up in BA's incubation spaces in 2018, with the rest being classifiable as ordinary businesses and self-employment (BA, 2019):

> Still, there is a lot of self-employment, people who, let's say, start up in their own businesses out of need, who create their own jobs because they cannot get these from others. We also continue to have many traditional activities, a lot of trade ... what we have done is to create a model that can respond to this disparity... we define our model inclusive (...) and intended to be universal and therefore to respond to the *existing* various types of entrepreneurial people. It must not be an exclusive model, either bottom-up or top-down. I mean that it is not exclusive in the sense of too technological or too elitist ... and how do we guarantee that? With what we offer. (Entrepreneurship Directorate, BA, October 2017)

Table 3.1 Entrepreneurial projects by sector supported by BA in 2018

	% of total
Commerce	17
Hospitality, tourism and leisure	15
Creative and cultural production	14
Business services	11
Personal services	8
ICT	8
Industry/manufacturing	8
Health and life sciences	5
Community and social services	3.9
Construction and urban planning services	3
Environment	2
Transport logistics	1

Source Annual Report, BA (2019)

Table 3.1 shows the way the inclusiveness principle leads to support for organisations working in very different economic sectors, but which somehow reflect the urban economy's plurality and, as we will see in subsequent chapters too, of the entrepreneurial profiles, experiences and motivations behind entrepreneurial choices.

3.3.2 *Embracing Heterogeneity: The Case of Milan*

In Milan the action taken to support ordinary entrepreneurship can be divided up into three categories. The first consists of support for new enterprise creation in the city's suburbs through municipal tenders. These calls for tenders are run by the municipality and draw on national funds allocated by the Ministry of Economic Development through a 1997 law envisaging action in support of entrepreneurship in deprived urban areas. Two major changes have been brought in since 2013. Firstly, while intervention of this sort initially provided hard support for the most part (economic incentives), it is now more hybrid in nature, providing accompanying services. For the duration of this research financial aid accounted for 50% of expenditure (the total expenditure envisaged in the "business plan" up to a maximum of one hundred thousand euros in any case) distributed as follows: a non-repayable contribution of up to 25% of the eligible total and planned expenditure and a subsidised loan for the remaining 25%. It also envisaged a municipal guarantee fund option set up with a view to facilitating access to further bank loans to finance the remaining 50% of expenditure. A second novelty concerned the target group. Although the entire working-age population was eligible, priority was given to young people up to the age of thirty-five and women.

The second of these categories is business microcredit, consisting of small loans granted to non-bankable households—those unable to access traditional credit channels—to support self-employment/entrepreneurial projects. It is managed by a non-profit organisation set up in 2011 and presided over by the city's mayor (hereafter "Foundation") comprising the Municipality of Milan, the Metropolitan City of Milan, the local chamber of commerce and the main Italian trade union confederations.[5] In 2012, the local government signed an agreement with the Foundation for the management of a guarantee fund and the activation of support services for microloans of up to EUR 25,000, partly with a view to launching a new microcredit circuit focusing on young people. The guarantee fund was intended to cover up to 75% of loans granted by banks. However, the Italian Ministry of Economic Development's creation of a national guarantee fund for SMEs accessing microcredit made the local guarantee fund obsolete. A new programme was, therefore, developed, on the one hand, to provide non-repayable financial contributions to reduce the interest levied by banks on nationally guaranteed microcredit and, on the other, to provide accompanying services.

The third is the Municipality of Milan's experimental launch of a number of spin-off projects in two municipal training schools in 2014, initially on the initiative of the teaching staff and headmasters of the schools themselves. The service targets students, who complete a course of study and specialisation (in graphic design, illustration, garden design, digital communication and web design among others). At the end of their schooling students can choose either a company internship or a supported self-employment/entrepreneurial project by a spin-off located within the school. For the first three years, the school provides students with free equipped spaces and laboratories (offices, meeting rooms, printers, etc.), a tutor, the opportunity for peer exchanges and continued contact with teachers. In many cases, this support results in initial running costs which are close to zero.

[5] The Italian General Confederation of Labour (CGIL), the Italian Confederation of Workers' Trade Unions (CISL) and the Italian Labour Union (UIL).

Worth noting, finally, are the series of initiatives that have grown up around these measures, including through partnerships between the various bodies. An example is an international project funded by the European programme YEP—Young Enterprise Program—developed together with the municipality, the Foundation, *FabriQ* (the Milan municipal social innovation incubator) and other local and overseas associations "to increase entrepreneurial opportunities for vulnerable young people in Milan, Lisbon and Madrid":

> the municipality proposed that we work together with FabriQ to create a partnership specialising in youth entrepreneurship and not only that, while FabriQ would benefit from our support, i.e. our greater ability to relate to the most vulnerable social groups. This means that the partnership we built sought to be as varied as possible. (Practitioner, NGO, Milan, February 2018)

In 2016 its various initiatives led to Milan being shortlisted as one of nine finalists for the European Capital of Innovation Award "for enhancing social inclusion and alternative models in the provision of public services to create more job opportunities" precisely by combining support for incubators and coworking with microcredit and inclusive entrepreneurship in general. These various initiatives have supported a number of businesses and aspiring entrepreneurs, within a single framework of support for start-ups:

> Including on the strength of the city's culture the municipality of Milan uses the term start-up to distinguish it from innovative start-ups, to encompass all emerging new businesses. It has a series of instruments, that you have probably already explored, which encourage the setting up of patisseries in the suburbs which cannot be described as innovative start-ups. (Expert and Policy advisor, Milan Municipality, March 2017)

An example of the wide ranging use of this term is one of the city's calls for proposals to support entrepreneurial projects in the city suburbs, entitled *Startupper. Enterprises in the Suburbs*, although the projects it supports are very different from *innovative* start-ups. Conjuring up start-up images (typically associated with innovative enterprises) in the context of ordinary entrepreneurship support programmes nurtures the notion that everyone might potentially identify with it, alongside the city's general business vocation. This associates entrepreneurship of whatever business type with the same symbolic value and social recognition. At the same time, it tends to obscure the differences behind entrepreneurship heterogeneity (discussed in Chapter 5). The way MESPs take the form of a differentiated set of programmes and instruments is of note, as it would seem—within the framework of inclusive entrepreneurship—to resonate with neoliberal city and start-up urbanism theories in so far as they value and promote self-entrepreneurship as an equally valid alternative for all. The next section will show, however, that promotion is not always the exclusive function of MESPs in the two cities.

3.4 Beyond Entrepreneurship Promotion

3.4.1 Barcelona: Alternative Views and Entrepreneurship Options

As Chapter 4 will explore further, entrepreneurship support programmes are not the exclusive preserve of innovative start-ups but also encompass individual coping strategies leveraging, precisely, on entrepreneurship. On the one hand, these coping strategies are taken for granted and supported as a viable alternative to employment, in line with the European normative framework. On the other hand, they are challenged by various social stakeholders, especially those public ones, e.g. Barcelona Activa:

> Especially in the case of youth programmes, it is important for us that participants know that this self-employment option exists. But also that their project not starting immediately is not a problem at all. This is the programme where we are least concerned about the business creation index, in the good sense of the word... (Consultant, St Augusti Convent, January 2018)

The caution regarding the results of the programmes—in terms of actual enterprise creation—that emerges from this interview extract highlights two elements commonly emerging from research. The first concerns the ambivalence around inclusive entrepreneurship. On the one hand, in fact, BA's aim is to ensure that these public policies and resources and the skills acquired over the years do not remain the preserve of higher-skilled, innovators, or the "elite", to use the words of an interviewee. On the other hand, attempting to guarantee equal opportunities to do business inevitably comes up against the risks inherent in it, which weigh more heavily on the shoulders of those who are not part of this elite (see also Chapter 5). However, in the face of this ambivalence, local actors, and public ones in particular, do not uncritically pursue enterprise creation whatever the cost, but counteract this ambivalence by eliciting reflection, for example, and sometimes dissuading some beneficiaries setting up in business.

Before enquiring further into this aspect, however, another important element must be taken into account, one which concerns the way in which Barcelona's entrepreneurship discourse has changed over the years together with the role local politics plays in it. A comparison of the latest local employment plans provides an insight into this change. Entrepreneurship is especially central to the *Pact for Local Employment 2008–2011* signed by Barcelona City Council with the main local trade unions and business organisations and Genralitat de Catalunya. Explicitly referring to the Lisbon agenda and the European Employment Strategy, the plan states that "Barcelona identifies entrepreneurship as a key factor in competitiveness, a tool with which to enhance the value of work, an employment driver, an innovation catalyst, a global positioning axis and an element of social and territorial cohesion", as well as "a professional, viable and future-oriented alternative for all" (p. 36, author's translation). Furthermore, the document states that "entrepreneurial, innovative and creative culture must permeate the city and requires promoting the identification of entrepreneurial initiative and creativity as an axis for the formation of Barcelona's future human capital, starting from the education system as a whole in its various levels" (p. 37). Conversely, the *Estrategia para el Empleo de Barcelona* for the 2016–2020 period fails even to mention entrepreneurship, and the same is true of business creation and self-employment, while it argues that "one of the main priorities of the new municipal government is the fight against unemployment and precariousness. Therefore, the promotion of quality employment for all will be one of the main form taken by the municipality's work" (p. 17).

The only exception to this is local youth employment plans which do generally feature entrepreneurship, albeit with certain differences. The Youth Employment Plan 2006–2019 symbolically entitled *El futuro de la Ocupación* describes the future of work in terms of technological and organisational innovation, new professions, new employment sectors, flexibility, small enterprises and, of course, self-employment (p. 22). However, entrepreneurship and self-employment also feature in the local *Pla per al Foment de l'Ocupació Juvenil de Qualitat 2016–2020* whose provisions include initiatives fostering the strengthening of young people's participation in BA's entrepreneurship support action, the promotion of tailor-made programmes and action to raise awareness of entrepreneurship through the integration of entrepreneurship in all facilities, programmes and services focusing on young people. An emphasis on social entrepreneurship is, however, also of note, with one of the plan's goals being to "promote knowledge of other economic forms, foster an active attitude to seeking out alternatives among the young, give the municipality's support to entrepreneurship initiatives, especially those of a collective nature and of social value" (p. 20, author's translation). As regards youth policies, both a tendency to adopt more transversal approaches in this policy area, i.e. to "present the whole spectrum of activities" (Employment Directorate, BA, December 2017) and an implicit consolidated assumption that young people are to be the privileged target of active policy approaches (Bifulco & Mozzana, 2016; Serrano Pascual & Martín Martín, 2017) is worth emphasising.

Overall, while in 2014 BA's declared mission was "to act as a reference point for policies oriented towards supporting business, create employment and project Barcelona internationally as an excellent environment for economic activity and social progress" (BA, 2014, p. 9), in 2017 its main aim was to "foment job opportunities, entrepreneurship and business support, as well as to respond to the needs of the local population from a plural, cooperative, social and solidarity economy perspective" (BA, 2017, p. 10).

This change reflects the intention of the new left-wing government elected in 2015 to distance itself from the conservative policy of its predecessor and, in general, from a vision of economic development focusing on growth and competitiveness. With this in mind, local government has tried to gradually shift its focus to promoting SSE, which includes support for appropriate forms of economic organisations (e.g. social cooperatives, collaborative civic platforms). As one interviewee pointed out: "the current government has introduced a key innovation that was never previously paid the attention it gets now (...) this means, more specifically, that cooperative or associative forms of entrepreneurship are accorded greater resources and political significance than in the past" (expert, Barcelona, October 2017). This policy is "totally new" according to the head of the SSE Directorate, and also differs from the pro-social entrepreneurship measures implemented by BA to varying degrees since the 1990s:

> This is a completely new policy (...) before there was something in Barcelona Activa... cautiously promoting cooperativism, you know, training

> courses or small training capsules, so that people who wanted to set up a business project would know that the legal formula of the cooperative existed, right? But there was no vision, or what was there was a complementary vision of the social economy, sometimes based on a charitable mentality… the new government decided to open a service department specific to the cooperative, social and solidarity economy. (SSE Directorate, Barcelona, April 2018)

The city administration's attempt to counterbalance its more conventional discourse on entrepreneurship reflects the different conceptions, ideas, values and political stances at play in this field. An anecdote of note in this regard concerns the news circulating during my Barcelona fieldwork in 2018 of a project which former delivery workers from large companies such as Deliveroo and Glovo were attempting to set up. The idea was to set up a food delivery cooperative in protest against prevalent sector working and contractual conditions and, at the same time, seeking to build an alternative business and social model. The project took shape in a SSE promotion space partly funded by Barcelona City Council. Interestingly, Glovo is one of BA's most successful start-up incubation success stories (along with companies such as Tiendeo, Privalia, Byhours). These contradictory visions of entrepreneurship and MESPs show that entrepreneurship and support strategies can be renegotiated at the local level.

Attempts to supplement consolidated Barcelona Activa activities focusing on the more conventional economy (the "big transatlantic liner") mainly relate to a strategy designed to ensure that these new measures and conceptions of entrepreneurship can gain the reputation and legitimacy that mainstream conceptions of entrepreneurship already possess:

> does this mean that the rest of Barcelona Activa was only working with the conventional economy? Yes, we are emphasising the fact that this did not exist before and strengthening it. It is not a matter of one against the other though. The other economy is continuing, to a greater or lesser extent (…) credibility has to be earned, that's where the challenge lies, it is a matter of transition. (SSE Directorate, Barcelona, April 2018)

The "gaining credibility" goal and thus consensus building around this new policy was pursued via the implementation of projects, but also by means of the opening in 2018 of a specific BA facility called InnoBA for

SSE support work and services. While support for the SSE is intended less to replace than to complement existing services, its addition to the compact and coherent start-up city image has, nonetheless, generated tensions arising from conflicting views of entrepreneurship:

> I think what the Barcelona City Council has done very well is to make Barcelona Activa a very powerful economic promotion institute in which factors such as technology and innovation are crucial. Or at least I would say that this was what was happening a couple of years ago, and this allowed us to create a technology hub, to create incubators, very powerful accelerators, to generate spaces in Barcelona such as the 22@ where there is also an urban plan that allows us to accommodate many companies and generate this technological factor. I would criticise the fact that for a couple of years, I think due to political ideology, that's what I think, this has slowed down. I think our drag factor comes from the good work done which has effectively avoided paralysis. Barcelona is still very attractive, there are many programmes, but it is trying to focus more on the social economy. The reason for my criticism is not that I don't believe in the social and collaborative economy, but it's a matter of competitivity and attractiveness (...) we are not so competitive in the social and collaborative economy (...) and we have made this the main municipal entrepreneurship policy priority of Barcelona City Council when there were others before! (Entrepreneurship Manager, BA Private Partner, Barcelona, October 2017)

However, this political shift has not been matched by a sharp reduction in BA's traditional services, which tend to coexist rather than compete with new ones. One of the main reasons for this lies in the strength of institutional legacies, i.e. a consolidated course of action revolving around attractiveness and market-based innovation, and of the local governance model characterised by the importance of public–private partnerships (Chapter 2). Another important reason is related to standard entrepreneurship services' capacity to support a key part of the urban economy, "Barcelona's commercial character, with its countless small shops owned and run by families with a strong local identity" (Garcia and Degen, p. 12, my translation). The capacity to intercept the social demands coming from the (independent) urban middle classes is also bound up with this:

> The city council of Barcelona knows that the city's dominant economic sector has a mercantile mindset (...) but most of its mercantile economy

> does not belong to multinationals, but to small and medium enterprises (…) which suffer from austerity, budgetary constraints, an absence of the necessary infrastructure… (SSE Directorate, Barcelona, April 2018)

These social demands include support for entrepreneurship, including in view of the fact that it is one of the strategies adopted by individuals to cope with labour market-related problems and not simply to seize new entrepreneurial opportunities (Chapter 4). Such strategies are not lacking in risk, especially in contexts where individuals are under growing pressure to take increasing responsibility for their own labour/social inclusion, to the extent of creating their own work. This has resulted in greater caution regarding the number of enterprises born from entrepreneurship support programmes in Barcelona:

> The idea of the programmes is that, at the end of the training period, participants will launch their business projects. This is the ideal. The indicators used to evaluate the success of entrepreneurship programmes are often the number of businesses created. This is the statistic that is of most interest. For us, it is very clear that this is not the indicator that… it is obviously important… but there's much more than that. All the projects not set up because participants didn't feel ready to go ahead… for whatever reason, it doesn't matter, but they didn't set up in business, for us this is an equally good indicator because it means, at least this is the view we give to this data, that there are people who have not risked what they would have risked by going ahead with their projects. They have not risked coming up against a brick wall. (Consultant, Sant Augusti Convent, Barcelona, January 2018)

The monitoring data I was shown after the interview evidenced that about 16% of young participants in the 2010–2016 period actually set up in business after the programme. At the end of this interview, it was suggested that I get in touch with one of those who took part in a past edition of the programme for under-30 aspiring entrepreneurs—unfortunately unable to take part in this research—who ultimately decided not to set up in business, and ended up getting a job at BA. This is clearly a unique case, but one which somehow exemplifies BA's integrated approach, i.e. that "one of the main tasks of a competent consultant is to orientate, to throw light on the weak points of a project and, at the same time, to suggest alternative paths" (Employment Directorate, BA, December 2017). In other words:

> We do not want people to *emprendan por emprender* [i.e. set up in business for the sake of it]. That is, our goal is not a quantitative one. Our goal is that those who want to set up a business can do so with the best chances of success. So, we want them to be trained, to properly assess their chances, to work on their business ideas. So, we don't look for... if a person approaches Barcelona Activa, what we try to do is to enhance analysis of the business idea, we want them to work on the idea... In all cases, what we try to ensure is that people coming to BA can access all useful resources in the fairest way possible, including to prevent them risking the few resources they have available too much, for example unemployment benefit. Because in Spain there is an option that consists of capitalising unemployment benefit, that is, those entitled to unemployment benefit can use it to start a business... of course, what we want is that... of course everyone is free to make their own decisions, but what we want is to direct all our resources to encouraging people to make this analysis, the business plan, and see if, with all the elements on the table, the project is feasible or risks not being economically viable. That is the purpose of all our resources. (Entrepreneurship Directorate, BA, October 2017)

Finally, it is worth mentioning that the municipality also took action to promote "service cooperatives by freelancers" in the wider *Pla d'Impuls de l'Economia Social i Solidària* (2016, p. 24):

> Self-employment is a matter of how you conceive it. In other words, individual entrepreneurship can sometimes be justified, but working alone can be more difficult, and our aim is to emphasise a collective vision and the value of cooperation. (...) For example, in relation to what I told you before about the study we did with people working in the informal economy, there is a very interesting project called Mujeres Pa'lante... most of these women are Latin American, they work as house cleaners or in hotels, they have formed an association and some are in the process of founding a cooperative (...) the fact that there is a public policy that talks about these issues, that puts them on the agenda, that develops funding mechanisms, that develops training processes... this is of help. (SSE Directorate, Barcelona, April 2018)

The local government thus aimed to give visibility to certain resistance practices from particularly exploited self-employed workers as well, leading to cooperation experiences designed to actively support this business model and try to resignify self-employment experiences in this way.

3.4.2 *Entrepreneurship in Milan: Supporting or Dissuading?*

While entrepreneurship in Barcelona is seen as a needing steering, whether to foster the city's competitivity and attractiveness in technological enterprise terms, to cope with the social vulnerability risks involved or as a tool to foster an alternative economic and social development agenda, Milan's dynamics differ from this in many respects. These differences are as much a matter of its urban governance model as of the political culture discussed in the previous chapter. More specifically, entrepreneurship support programmes tend to be portrayed as a necessary response to the erosion of standard employment (i.e. long-term job security, full-time hours, social benefits and other standards associated with stable employment) and, therefore, as a phenomenon to be "accompanied" rather than "governed":

> If the municipality has a goal, as regards employment policy, it is at a crossroads: what do I do? Do I encourage traditional forms of work, or do I decide to promote new entrepreneurial programmes? Our basic assumption has always been that it is hard to believe that traditional forms of work, the steady job, the open-ended contract, can be the answer to the huge employment gap we have at the moment. Therefore, we decided, in the face of this crossroads, to reward and support those who want to create their own jobs, in some way. (Economic planning unit, Milan Municipality, April 2017)

Particularly where young people are concerned, the prevailing idea is that they are increasingly committed to seeking out, and constructing, their own individual path through labour working conditions and, because of this, increasingly attracted to entrepreneurship. This state of affairs seems to be taken for granted as an argument for a pragmatic response. On this point, in a 2014 public speech the city councillor for the urban economy and labour stated that: "the crisis has also shown us that there is a new propensity to do business in the younger generations. Whether this is the result of constraints or a natural propensity is, at this time, of secondary importance".[6] There would seem to be general consensus around this approach among respondents. For example, in the creative and knowledge economy sectors, entrepreneurship tends to

[6] TEDx held in Milan, 11 February 2014. https://www.youtube.com/watch?v=xlgJdrj6DKA (accessed: 03 July 2023).

be understood as an inevitable answer to the rise of self-employment/entrepreneurship as one privileged form of work among others:

> outside of the economic crisis of recent years, this is a sector [illustration and graphic design] where freelancers predominate. So, if these young people do not experiment with the opportunity to develop it [this kind of path] ... this would, in my opinion, be a limit for them. (Teacher, municipal school spin-off, Milan, April 2017)

This respondent's view is that the growth of self-employment in these areas is also moving step by step with young people's growing preference for it:

> our students increasingly enter the labour market less as employees than self-employed. So, it's true that we still help a lot of people do internships, and a lot of people find a standard job, *like my grandfather's, to be clear*. But the job market is increasingly embracing new forms of work such as freelancing, which is, by the way, also appreciated by the very same individuals. (Principal, municipal school spin-off, Milan, April 2017)

On the one hand, this approach is consistent with the depoliticised nature of the policies and discourses revolving around entrepreneurship, where the political dimension tends to be masked in favour of celebrations of entrepreneurship's inherently positive contribution to economic development and social progress (Essers et al., 2017). On the other hand, it reflects the way local governments have dealt with the (unexpected) problems raised by the implementation of these policies, in a way that accords with the pragmatism characteristic of the local policy tradition (Chapter 2):

> The approach we've always taken is to support new businesses with the potential to hire new workers because, clearly, if a business is solid and has good bases, it is able to grow and create employment, which is what we all want. But everyone being turned into entrepreneurs is a problem we have had to face because we realised that many people are embarking on this... (Self-Entrepreneurship and Microfinance Service Directorate, Milan Municipality, April 2017)

This interview excerpt highlights a key point pertaining to the ambivalence engendered by policy instruments' implicit and explicit goals, on the one hand, and the municipal mandate to respond to citizens' needs and demands while helping to stem social vulnerability exacerbated by individualisation processes, on the other. In the case of its calls for tenders, the municipality reacted to this situation by bringing in what have been called "pre-calls", preparatory courses prior to calls for new businesses in peripheral areas designed to prepare people for entrepreneurship, with a focus on the risks involved in it, and the introduction of compulsory mentoring services. The interviewee continues:

> The idea of anticipating our tenders with pre-call, providing in-depth discussions or seminars, is due to the fact that we felt it was necessary to clarify the process they are getting into with entrepreneurs. And in fact after this phase, many give up. In the pre-call we give all available information about what it means to do business. This is a key change from previous municipal tenders where this step was simply not taken.

Still in a pragmatic vein, the selection process would seem to be viewed by the municipality as an effective way to help address the social risks associated with self-entrepreneurship by discouraging it in certain cases. As a respondent explained:

> If I want to open a bakery but have never worked in a bakery and have never even attended a baking course, then my business plan is a bit baseless. Or it's not completely baseless if maybe I have a partner who is or has been a baker, so I can have the management and administrative skills and she can have the craft skills, and together we're fine. But if I want to open on my own and I have no idea how to do it, the project loses its value, so to speak. (Consultant, municipal tenders, Milan, February 2017)

Of note here is that selection almost always comes with hybrid support for entrepreneurship, i.e. support which includes economic incentives. The OECD, for example, recommends that: "intensive support should be competitive or filtered to select recipients that are motivated and most likely to succeed", while "extensive support should be low cost and offered widely" (OECD, 2016, p. 20). In this view, the aim is to channel higher spending measures into projects with the best chance of survival, thus turning public spending into a productive investment.[7] However, as we have seen, local public actors would seem, to some extent, to be resignifying and redirecting the public selection process towards alternative goals. But what criteria is this selection based on? Many respondents (in Barcelona, too) see the chances of success on which selection is based as having little to do with the availability of funds, because political intervention is expected to compensate for the lack of individual economic resources (a point explored further in Chapter 5). By contrast, greater emphasis is placed on individual capabilities, including previous experience—as the interview extract shown above demonstrates—as well as entrepreneurial drive: "we assess the entrepreneur and the entrepreneurial project … the entrepreneur in terms of skills […] skills do not necessarily have to be high but, of course, you have to prove you have the necessary skills or a willingness to acquire them and improve" (Consultant, municipal tenders, Milan, February 2017).

Selection processes based on chances of success show logic hybridisation. One of these is the idea that these policies' "success" should be measured by survival rates, with 3- or 5-year survival rates being the main indicators by which the effectiveness and legitimacy of such measures are assessed. On the other hand, selection is seen as a means of pragmatically limiting the risks—less business than social—associated with entrepreneurial initiative in times of individualisation. It should be noted, however, that selection tells us nothing about the fate of those at the bottom of the list, the excluded. What happens to those who do not benefit from municipal hybrid support? Do they still go on to set up in business? While the "pre-calls" referred to above do indeed seem to help discourage some from pursuing their plans, what happens in other cases? While I cannot answer these questions here, what I can do is point to the risks involved in providing support only to the less in need, by enhancing the accumulation of advantages involved in professional experience and soft skills. The fact that those whose chances of success are lower may need diversified or alternative support reinforces the risk involved in abandoning such people rather than providing them with the extra guidance and support they need, which may be less entrepreneurial than holistic. Such risks would seem potentially to have been reduced in Barcelona,

[7] This accords with the basic principles of the social investment paradigm inspiring the reorganisation of European welfare states. For a more in-depth discussion of this, see Morel et al. (2012).

due both to the existence of soft supports to entrepreneurship, open to everyone, and the BA's policy and tool integration.

3.5 Inclusive MESPs: from Top-Down Dynamics to Agency

This chapter has highlighted the fact that MESPs do not simply reflect the ways in which growth and competitiveness paradigms have redefined urban policy and governance under the more general influence of neoliberal thinking. They are also an example of how—even in a field which might be seen as paradigmatic of the neoliberal ethos—both top-down dynamics enacted by local actors and alternative logics not always consistent with neoliberal value or competitiveness goals are at work. The form taken by top-down dynamics at the local level also varies by context. First of all, local models of governance, institutional legacies, politics and local political cultures matter. We have seen this both in Barcelona, where entrepreneurial and competitive logics are hybridised with social transformation goals on these grounds and forms of resistance, reflecting conflicts between different conceptions of MESPs, and in Milan. In line with Milan's governance model, politics remain in the background here but research has once again cast light on the way the significance of local actor role in this field is being renegotiated in the face of the contradictions associated with inclusive entrepreneurship. However differently, both cases show that entrepreneurship is not just fostered but also hindered by attempts to reduce the risks involved and negotiate the ambivalence and contradictions associated with inclusive entrepreneurship. This is particularly evident in contexts of increasing individualisation, where pressures toward self-entrepreneurship risk exacerbating social vulnerabilities.

While urban entrepreneurialism and neoliberal city theories may elucidate the discourse, symbol and practices surrounding the homogenisation evident in the dissemination of the start-up city model as an ideal to strive for, we have seen that such processes are relevant but subject to limited recontextualisation by public institutions and social actor agency. The latter falls into either Katz's oppositional, or resistance—to their use and involving readjustment (2004; Chapter 1) by shaping policies (and voicing practices) oriented to generating alternative economic models, such as the social and solidarity economy (Barcelona)—or resilience categories, through small-scale strategies and the pragmatic interweaving of a range of tools, objectives and logics (Milan). In both cases, MESPs face an "everyday city" which is also commercial in nature and a fragmented socioeconomic fabric. This is important, because "start-up cities" are deemed to actually moves in the direction of disembedded economies and forms of enterprise, privileging "inclusion in global networks and flows of ideas, discourses, knowledge, and technical skills" (Rossi & Di Bella, 2017, p. 1005). Looking at the start-up city holistically, this chapter (and this book) shows that the reality is more multifaceted and only partly reflects such dynamics. It is also impacted by social structures based on the independent and, to some extent impoverished, middle class that is typical of the "European city" model (Le Galès, 2016) and which has helped shape a local culture of entrepreneurship, beyond the neoliberal business culture, that is now intertwined with new drives, meanings and strategies, as we will see in the next chapter.

References

Amin, A., & Thrift, N. (2007). Cultural-economy and cities. *Progress in Human Geography, 31*(2), 143–161.

Arum, R., & Müller, W. (2004). *The reemergence of self-employment: A comparative study of self-employment dynamics and social inequality*. Princeton University Press.

Barcelona Activa. (2014). *Memoria de Actividades 2014*. Barcelona Activa.

Barcelona Activa. (2017). *Activities Report 2017*. Barcelona Activa.

Barcelona Activa. (2019). *Memòria d'Activitats 2018*. Barcelona Activa.

Barcelona Activa. (2020). *Barcelona. Datasheet 2020*. Barcelona: Barcelona Activa.

Bifulco, L. (2017). *Social policies and public action*. Routledge.

Bifulco, L., & Mozzana, C. (2016). Introduzione: oltre l'employability. Approcci e prospettive per le transizioni giovanili scuola-lavoro. *Sociologia del lavoro, 141*(1), 7–22.

Borghi, P., & Murgia, A. (2019). Between precariousness and freedom: The ambivalent condition of independent professionals in Italy. In W. Conen & J. Schippers (Eds.), *Self-employment as precarious work: A European perspective* (pp. 132–152). Edward Elgar.

Borghi, V. (2011). One-way Europe? Institutional guidelines, emerging regimes of justification, and paradoxical turns in European welfare capitalism. *European Journal of Social Theory, 3*, 321–341.

D'Ovidio, M. (2016). *The creative city does not exist. Critical essays on the creative and cultural economy of cities*. Ledizioni.

Essers, C., Dey, P., Tedmanson, D., & Verduyn, K. (2017). *Critical perspectives on entrepreneurship. Challenging dominant discourses*. Routledge.

Eurocities. (2013). *Cities supporting inclusive entrepreneurship*. Eurocities.
Eurofond. (2017). *Exploring self-employment in the European Union*. Publications Office of the European Union.
European Commission. (2013). *Entrepreneurship 2020 Action Plan – Reigniting the entrepreneurial spirit in Europe*, COM(2012) 795, Brussels.
European Commission. (2014). *Activating jobseekers through entrepreneurship: Start-up incentives in Europe*. European Union.
Eurostat. (2022a). *Business demography statistics*, retrieved from: https://ec.europa.eu/eurostat/statistics-explained/index.php?title=Business_demography_statistics (accessed 01/07/2023).
Eurostat. (2022b). *Structural business statistics overview*, retrieved from: https://ec.europa.eu/eurostat/statistics-explained/index.php?title=Structural_business_statistics_overview#Sectoral_analysis (accessed 01/07/2023).
Fellini, I. (2010). L'articolazione del lavoro indipendente nell'assetto post-industriale. *Sociologia del lavoro* (118), 169–182.
Foucault, M. (2005). *Nascita della Biopolitica*. Feltrinelli.
Gallino, L. (1978). *Dizionario di Sociologia*. Utet.
GEM. (2023). *Global Entrepreneurship Monitor 2022/2023 global report: Adapting to a "new normal."* GEM.
Katz, C. (2004). *Growing Up Global. Economic Restructuring and Children's Everyday Lives*. University of Minnesota Press.
Le Galès, P. (2016). Neoliberalism and Urban Change: Stretching a Good Idea Too Far?, *Territory, Politics, Governance*, *4*(2), 154–172.
Lodigiani, R., & Scippa, E. (2014). Il self-employment tra politiche del lavoro e occupazionali, nella prospettiva europea dell'attivazione. In P. A. Varesi & A. Vergani (Eds.), *Self-employment e Sostegno Pubblico all'Imprenditorialità* (pp. 227–266). Franco Angeli.
Marchesnay, M. (2012). Innovations, territoires et capitalisme entrepreneurial. *Marché et organisations* (16), 181–208.
Milan Chamber of Commerce. (2020). *Milano Produttiva 2020*. Pearson Italia.
Morel, N., Palier, B., & Palme, J. (2012). *Towards a social investment welfare state? Ideas, policies and challenges*. Policy Press.
OECD. (2016). *Supporting youth entrepreneurship in Italy*. OECD Publishing.
OECD/European Commission. (2017). *The Missing Entrepreneurs 2017. Policies for inclusive entrepreneurship*. OECD Publishing.
OECD/European Commission. (2019). *The Missing Entrepreneurs 2019*. OECD Publishing.
OECD/European Commission. (2021). *The Missing Entrepreneurs 2021*. OECD Publishing.
Pill, M. (2021). *Governing cities: Politics and policy*. Palgrave Macmillan.

Pirone, F. (2023). Imprenditorialità e società capitalistiche. In E. Morlicchio & A. Cocorullo (Eds.), *Dieci lezioni di sociologia economica* (pp. 57–72). Franco Angeli.

Rossi, U., Di Bella, A. (2017). Start-up urbanism: New York Rio de Janeiro and the global urbanization of technology-based economies, *Environment and Planning A: Economy and Space 49*(5), 999–1018.

Sassen, S. (2006). *Cities in a world economy*. Pine Forge Press.

Scalise, G. (2020). *The political economy of policy ideas. The European strategy of active inclusion in context*. Palgrave Macmillan.

Serrano Pascual, A., & Martín Martín, P. (2017). From "employability" to "entrepreneuriality" in Spain: Youth in the spotlight in times of crisis. *Journal of Youth Studies, 20*(7), 798–821.

Swedberg, R. (2000). The social science view of entrepreneurship: Introduction and practical applications. In R. Swedberg (Ed.), *Entrepreneurship: The social science view* (pp. 7–44). Oxford University Press.

Torri, R. (2017). Milan. Challenging the private interest government in times of austerity. In R. Cucca & C. Ranci (Eds.), *Unequal cities: The challenge of post-industrial transition in times of austerity*. Routledge.

van Berkel, R., & Møller, H. I. (2002). *Active social policies in the EU*. The Policy Press.

Woodman, D. (2013). Researching 'ordinary' young people in a changing world: The sociology of generations and the 'missing middle' in youth research. *Sociological Research Online, 18*(1), 179–190.

CHAPTER 4

"The Mindset Has Changed a Lot"? Situated Agency of Youth Entrepreneurs

Abstract This chapter provides insights into MESPs in Barcelona and Milan from the perspective of their young beneficiaries. It explores young people's subjective experiences and meaning and value attribution, interpreted as influenced by broader socio-economic and institutional changes, as well as the result of differing ways of adapting to such changes and of meaningful context-sensitive reframing processes. The focus is on the circumstances in which the decision to set up in business emerges, the relationship with the local labour market, the role of the family and representations of entrepreneurship. As well as highlighting the discourse, symbol and practice standardisation processes at work the chapter examines the way young beneficiaries resignify the entrepreneurial device within their coping strategies in individualised contexts.

Keywords Inclusive entrepreneurship · Youth entrepreneurship · Situated agency · Coping strategies · Barcelona · Milan · Start-up ideology

Previous chapters have highlighted that municipal entrepreneurship support policies (MESPs), on the one hand, reflect the way growth and competitiveness paradigms have reframed urban policies and governance under the broader influence of neoliberal thought and, on the other,

M. Dodaro, *Unpacking the 'Start-up City'*,
https://doi.org/10.1007/978-3-031-50212-5_4

illuminated different, at times contradictory, dynamics. This chapter will explore these dynamics and contradictions by giving space to young people's subjective experiences and meaning and value attribution, interpreted as influenced by broader socio-economic and institutional changes, as well as the result of differing ways of adapting to such changes and of meaningful context-sensitive reframing processes. While urban policies and models of governance contribute to shaping the context within which people's actions and aspirations take shape, people themselves play a part in this as well. They, too, bring ideas, values, needs, resources and strategies, thereby contributing to informing policies and shaping local social, economic, political and cultural specificities. They are not mere endpoints in processes playing out above their heads while determining their actions. This is the starting assumption of a chapter that examines MESPs from the perspective of their beneficiaries, with a focus on the circumstances in which the decision to set up in business emerges, the relationship with the local labour market, the role of the family and representations of entrepreneurship. Its results show a very detailed portrait of the different meanings entrepreneurship takes on and how these are intertwined with the specificities of the two contexts, contributing to showing that local actors do not simply replicate mainstream conceptions of entrepreneurship. In this regard, and not least, I will also critically discuss the idea—widespread among interviewees, including the young themselves—of the growing involvement of the very young in business creation, portrayed as unwitting victims of political-cultural policies whose aim is to improve their engagement and responsibility by increasing their self-entrepreneurship.

4.1 Cities as Ideal Opportunity Entrepreneur Milieux

As is widely known, contemporary cities are packed with entrepreneurial opportunities. Jane Jacobs (1970) emphasised the relevance of cities to economic development processes and their ability to generate economic diversity and innovation last century. The city is thus mostly depicted as a place of opportunity-based entrepreneurship. In the scientific literature, this category is used to identify entrepreneurial initiative whose genesis lies primarily in recognising market opportunities, as opposed to necessity-driven entrepreneurship driven by an absence of alternatives (Sheehan & Namara, 2015). These two categories correspond to two differing images of both entrepreneurship and entrepreneurs themselves. An entrepreneur pursuing an opportunity is indeed first and foremost a free, creative, independent individual incapable, for this very reason, of fitting into ordinary contexts, such as hierarchical and bureaucratic organisations. "True" entrepreneurs of this sort are not afraid to "break" free of standard employment, with the protection and rights which come with this, to bring their dreams to fruition. In Schumpeterian terms, such people are special, not entirely homo economicus, insofar as they are motivated less by rational and utilitarian reasons—as they are lacking in the information required for a purely rational assessment of costs and benefits—than by a desire to get rich, a will to win, for success and the joy of creation (Schumpeter, 1947). They are also seen as agents of change, as well as desocialised individuals whose choices, behaviours and success are attributed to special personality traits and merits.

While opportunity-driven entrepreneurship is portrayed as the result of free choice and connoted positively, need-driven entrepreneurship is generally seen as the outcome of external constraints (economic crisis, unemployment rates, social protection deficits) and bound up with very modest earnings and growth expectations, and mere survival strategies. Accordingly, it is the picture least advertised and emphasised in the public entrepreneurship discourse, in which the stress is mainly on the wealthy and successful entrepreneur archetype, typically a white man, as embodied by the new start-up aesthetic of entrepreneur-innovators such as Steve Jobs, Mark Zuckerberg and Elon Musk, also popularised in movies, TV shows and books (Luise, 2019).

The start-up rhetoric has also contributed to the construction of entrepreneurship as an increasingly democratic phenomenon and, partly because of this, as within the reach of younger people too (see also Chapter 5). Steve Jobs was 21 when he founded Apple Computers, Mark Zuckerberg was 20 when he launched Facebook (and already a billionaire at 23), while Elon Musk began his entrepreneurial career at 24 when he set up a web software company. The fact that they funded their businesses by raising capital from financial investors or, in the case of Steve Jobs, by selling a minibus, has further fuelled the belief that entrepreneurship in contemporary society is within the reach of anyone with an idea and a great deal of determination and dedication, to a greater extent than in the past. Moreover, the image of young people as innovative, creative and socialised early to labour insecurity (at least those not stigmatised as idlers) has helped reinforce this idea and the stereotype by which it is young people who are best suited to seizing most modern entrepreneurial opportunities, especially those generated by the advent of new technologies. Furthermore, the appeal of self-fulfilment, opportunity, success, merit and enterprise is seen as more attractive to young people who are viewed, on the one hand, as having already internalised entrepreneurship aspirations and patterns and, on the other hand, as living in "neoliberal cities" and thus further prompted "to see themselves as individualized and active subjects responsible for enhancing their own well-being" (Larner, 2000, in Pinson & Morel Journel, 2017, p. 6; see also Rossi, 2017; Sternberg, 2023).

However, the sociological literature has shown how little such ideal models are actually present in representations of young people, seen as "being at the intersection of structuring social processes that configure their lives and dynamics of subjectivity which make them competent reflexive social actors able to assign meanings to their practices, choices and trajectories" (Nico & Caetano, 2021, p. 3). Drawing on the concept of "situated agency" (Evans, 2002; Chapter 1), the aim of this and the subsequent chapter is to explore the interplay between structural constraints and agency by analysing the experiences of those involved in MESPs as beneficiaries, starting from the circumstances by which they decide to go into business and by which entrepreneurship becomes a concretely viable option, with a specific focus on context-sensitive economic, social and political-cultural dimensions. The focus will also be on their perceptions of youth entrepreneurship phenomenon and the extent to which they identify with it. Their relationship to the resources mobilised within MESPs will be only briefly mentioned as it will be explored further in the next chapter.

This analysis also draws on sociological approaches to the study of entrepreneurship suggesting that its drivers are varied and located at the intersection of dynamics cutting across multiple system encompassing cultural, economic, labour market and family factors (see Chapter 1).

4.2 Not So Young?

In a public speech in 2014 the then councillor for Milan's Urban Economy and Employment argued that "the crisis has shown us that there is a new propensity for doing business in the younger generations, whether this is a result of constraints or a natural propensity is currently of secondary importance".[1] The idea of increased interest among young people in self-employment and entrepreneurship has also featured in many interviews with key professionals, according to whom young people are now considering alternatives to wage employment to a greater extent than in the past. But who are these "young people"? Challenges inherent in the transition to adulthood in countries such as Italy and Spain, in particular, have made identifying clear boundaries between one stage of life and the next especially problematic and uncertain (De Luigi, 2007). The category of young adults, generally made up of the under 35s, seeks precisely to account for these countries' extended understanding of the transition to adulthood, linked to delayed entry to the labour market and consequently leaving the parental home and forming one's own household. Entrepreneurship itself may be a reason to postpone certain milestones in the transition to adulthood. This is the case, for example, of Roberto,[2] a 33-year-old entrepreneur interviewed in Milan, who decided to put off leaving his parental home in order to devote his financial resources and time to his entrepreneurial plans. As a result, the age limits applying to youth entrepreneurship programmes differ, sometimes targeting the under 30s and sometimes the under 35s.

Data from the Global Entrepreneurship Monitor (reported OECD/ European Commission, 2019) shows that almost half of young Europeans aged 18–30 declared an interest in entrepreneurship in the 2014–2018 period. However, the same data highlighted that just 4.7% actively sought to set up in business in same time period. About 13% of the labour force were self-employed in the EU in 2021, a percentage that is about twice as high as total numbers of young people (5.9%), but with higher shares of self-employment recorded in Slovakia (13.8%), Italy (12%) and Greece (11.1%), while Spain's rates were in line with the European average (Eurostat, 2022). Overall, the largest segment was the 30–49 age group (52.7% in Italy, 53.4 in Spain, and 51.5% in the EU as a whole) (OECD, 2020).

In this context, the capacity of MESPs to attract the young has proved to be limited and the 30–35 age group was seen as making a difference by many interviewees, despite the growth of symbolic and material incentives

[1] TEDx held in Milan, 11 February 2014, https://www.youtube.com/watch?v=3RC1ZWJ1r8s (accessed: 19 July 2023).

[2] Invented names were given to research participants to preserve anonymity.

for youth entrepreneurship. For example, Barcelona Activa's programme targeting the under 30s:

> This is actually a programme for which it is more difficult to find participants. But we think this is due to its age limit - open only to the under-30s - because some programmes include the under 35s and, well, in those five years you can see the difference... whilst under 30s are very young. They are people who are at the following stages of life: studying, or starting their first job. In other words, at this age they are not thinking much about setting up their own businesses and it is more difficult to find people with an idea they want to develop. (Consultant, Sant Agustí Convent, January 2018)

As a result, the young entrepreneurs taking part in this research (34) were predominantly young adults whose average age was 30.5 (29.5 in Milan and 33 in Barcelona). Almost all of the respondents had completed their studies and most had already worked for some years. They generally attached value to their prior work experience, and, if they had gone straight from university into entrepreneurship, they saw this as a shortcoming. This is consistent with evidence from other studies showing that entrepreneurship usually follows a few years of work (Aldrich, 2005). Entrepreneurship tends thus to be carefully thought out and, as we will shortly see, a way in which the young people interviewed rework their labour market experiences, express their abilities to make decisions and incorporate them into their own frames of meaning.

4.3 Innovators

The paths, strategies and motivations of the young interviewees involved in setting up or consolidating an innovative enterprise differed from the other interviewees in several respects. First of all, a number of their socio-biographical characteristics differed. In gender terms, the sample was largely made up of men (15 out of 21). Getting women involved in this research was made more difficult by the gender gap existing in the world of innovative start-ups (Manzo & Pais, 2017; OECD/European Commission, 2019). The gender gap in entrepreneurship rates is generally to be explained on historical, socio-economic and cultural grounds. In the specific case of innovative start-ups, it also seems to be a matter of lower numbers of women studying STEM subjects at university (OECD/

European Commission, 2019). Indeed, educational background would seem to play a very important part in entrepreneur-innovator biographies (Manzo & Pais, 2017). In this research sample, only two of the interviewees were not graduates. According to policy stakeholder interviews, this data reflects a broader profile of young people supported within the various innovative start-up services and programmes offered in Barcelona and Milan. It should also be borne in mind that education levels tend to be higher in European cities than in other areas (European Commission, 2016).

More specifically, most interviewees had technical-scientific or economic backgrounds, while only four were humanities and social sciences graduates. The former skills would seem to be particularly well suited to seizing economic opportunities in the digital era as the projects involved are mostly in the digital economy and platform spheres (including e-commerce, the sharing economy, digital services). With a few exceptions for those with a humanities background, interviewees setting up innovative start-up had generally not experienced any specific barriers to entering the labour market. Although many cities in (Mediterranean and Eastern) Europe have high unemployment rates, both Barcelona and Milan offer a relatively high number of employment opportunities and the demand for highly qualified labour is significant (European Commission, 2016). In such contexts, entrepreneurship tends to be less need driven and the nascent entrepreneurs interviewed seemed to fit easily into the opportunity-driven entrepreneur category. The in-depth interviews show a more complex and nuanced picture, however.

4.3.1 Innovators for Innovation's Sake

Some of the young innovators interviewed were in the process of developing promising projects which received sizeable funding from specialised investors. In some cases, they were already well down the path to consolidation and successful enough to have been invited to speak about their experiences and sometimes to mentor other nascent entrepreneurs, typically by the incubators they themselves attended. They shared extremely high levels of economic, social and cultural capital and their motives seemed to have had little to do with previous work experience, or employment-related concerns. Barcelona-born Marc set up his company at the age of about 31 and had just turned 35 when I interviewed him:

> I studied business administration here in Barcelona, and then I started working immediately in the marketing field, in multinational companies. After 5/6 years of experience, I did an MBA in Barcelona, it was a moment of... "stop and think". It was a full-time MBA, so I left my job. However, I had a very clear idea of training to set up my own company. I really wanted to be an entrepreneur. I was lucky that during the MBA I met my two co-founders, we made friends. (...) The company was born from a highly interactive and planned brainstorming process in which we analysed various ideas and business models that worked in other countries.

Pau, 34, was from Barcelona. We met at Barcelona Activa (BA) where he rented a space together with his business partner to develop a visual commerce and marketing platform:

> I studied economics here at the University of Barcelona, I did an exchange in England and one in the United States during my university career. After my studies I worked as a business consultant in one of the main Spanish consulting companies, and four years later I set up a new business consulting unit with colleagues. It was an intrapreneurship project within the company, and I worked there for another two years as a consultant. Then the company we set up this business unit at bought human resources software and I was made general manager of this software, and I stayed there for almost three years. Then I started working on this company with my partner...

For both Marc and Pau the transition from university education to employment was smooth and their entrepreneurial choices do not seem to have been bound up with their job record or a lack of career opportunities within the companies employing them. It rather took shape within especially favourable socialisation contexts provided by specific educational and training paths and their peer group. In Pau's case, it is worthy of note that companies themselves sometimes provide fertile terrain for the development of entrepreneurial skills, involving employees directly in the creation of new business initiatives. Moreover most interviewees had at least one close family member with entrepreneurship experience, which makes the family of origin another particularly important context in socialisation to entrepreneurship:

> I actually benefitted from coming from a family of entrepreneurs, which made me aware of what it meant to do business, of the fact that there is

> a wonderful and precious phase in which value, employment, is generated and that you work harder than ever before, more than anywhere else. My father has his own business, my grandparents also owned their companies, I come from a very favourable environment from this point of view, close to the world of business and entrepreneurship. (Marc)

In contrast to what one might expect, recognising a market opportunity does not seem to have played a decisive role here. This is arguably important when the decision to actually set up in business is taken, but not when an entrepreneurial career is planned. On the one hand, the existence of business opportunities there for the taking seems to be taken for granted. Both the local context and a more general discourse regarding the growth opportunities offered by the knowledge economy, new technologies and the availability of resources of various kinds accessible in the *start-up city* certainly played an important part in this. On the other hand, business experience seems to be actively sought out, with aims being becoming an entrepreneur or simply getting rich. Marc's case—with a business idea which emerged from a brainstorming process specifically designed to find an idea to implement—is emblematic of the way the desire to be an entrepreneur may predate the economic opportunity itself. Among these interviewees, the idea itself, the entrepreneurial project, seems to have been less an end in itself than a means by which to achieve individual success, enrichment and social status ambitions. In addition, it should be borne in mind that, as other studies have also found (Luise, 2019), entrepreneurial ideas themselves are often seen as secondary determinants of success, since start-ups operate in a context of radical uncertainty. Consistent with the individualisation processes that entrepreneurship fully embodies, what is deemed to make the difference is teamwork and design, planning and working skills (in jargon, *execution*): "the only key to success is execution... the idea gets copied, in the end there are many things that competitors can copy, the only thing they can't do like you is the execution part, your work, the hours you spend on it, the effort you put in, how you persuade a team to commit to the project all the same" (Marc).

It is to this that respondents attributed the positive feedback they had received from financial investors who had, on occasions, provided them with substantial funding. Marc had worked as part of a team to create a digital platform that soon became a high growth start-up, not least as a result of it having obtained around "6 million euros of funding, from international, local and public investors". These were resources which sped up the growth of a company based in Barcelona but already with branches in Mexico, Colombia and Chile.

> I: *Then I don't know if I can exactly consider you a start-upper, and the company a start-up, what do you think?* A: Well, we are now a consolidated company, but we have retained our start-up spirit because... the company concept is, I think, for much more consolidated businesses, in very mature markets... with little growth, little innovation (...) it's true that in a consolidated company you can be equally enterprising and innovative, just like us... you can have the same start-up spirit that we have (...) I think my company has a start-up spirit, even though we have revenues in the millions and offices, we have finance, we are profitable. The reality is that our operations are the same as any other company's, but we have retained the freshness, innovation and ability to move fast that a start-up has.

The explicit and implicit values at stake in the start-up realm would seem to wield significant influence in such cases. As this extract also suggests, the start-up concept is much more than simply identifying specific types of enterprises or their early stages. The enthusiasm for innovative entrepreneurship, the value of novelty, change and growth as opposed to stability and preservation: these are all elements in start-ups' symbolic and value mosaic (Luise, 2019).

These values often include something of an entrepreneur-innovator personality cult and sometimes an explicitly negative view of regular employment which, in some cases, young entrepreneur-innovators have never contemplated. This is true of Francesco, 24, originally from southern Italy, who first moved to Rome to attend a BSc in economics and then to Milan where he initially enrolled on an MSc in economics and business strategies before realising that "it was not giving me what I was looking for". So Francesco signed up for an intensive business start-up course during which he started working on a sharing economy marketplace (connecting suppliers and owners of specific equipment with people interested in renting them). Francesco ruled out working as an employee:

> I: *have you had any work experience?* R: I was product manager in my family's company, but if you mean employed, no, because I'm in the company there too... so no, I've never had that kind of experience, and I would also say... I never will! (...) I want to create conditions that can

generate value, that's my ambition, to generate value for those around me... because it's very rewarding, then obviously because it generates a lot of value for yourself too (...) but in general, I don't intend to *timbrare il cartellino* and I never will.

The Italian expression *timbrare il cartellino* is generally used to refer to routine nine-to-five jobs, and reflects Francesco's negative attitude to standard employment,[3] with its assumption that it leaves the way open for cheating and opportunistic behaviour by employees. Partly in line with the local cultural models outlined in Chapter 2 (emphasising the value of private initiative and laissez-faire policy approaches), Francesco tends overall to reject state authority and its tax and labour regulatory functions, in particular, which he sees as interfering with freedom of enterprise and holding back innovative companies:

they shouldn't make us pay taxes in the short term, at least if the person [the employee hired] agrees [to work without social security contributions], because I assure you that we pay him the same amount, but we give him all the money... consider that if it makes a big difference to me whether a person earns 1,000 or 1,300 (...) we're not a company with a turnover of millions (...) the tax burden doesn't allow me to pay more people or pay them more and go faster... and if I don't go at certain speeds I might be overwhelmed by other players. (...) the 2.0 economy requires adjustments to the system, because we are no longer at Olivetti (...) if Foodora hadn't had a tax problem, there wouldn't have been that fuss about the guys... now, if deliverers are doing it as a full-time job, that's another problem (...) these guys want to be hired indefinitely to ride a bike! but Foodora... maybe they would even hire them, but it would cost them a boatload of money which, for obvious reasons, would no longer make its growth sustainable.

In this view the entrepreneur is portrayed as a kind of hero with a singular propensity for taking responsibility and working hard:

[3] The term "standard employment" refers to the traditional employment relationship characterised by a set of standard features and protection which typically include a full-time work schedule, job security, regular working hours, a stable salary or wage, and access to employment benefits such as health insurance, retirement plans and paid time off.

> what we do, it brings it home to you how hard life is in some respects. It places responsibility on you, then a series of unforeseen events, problems... which change you. I: *How do you mean*? A: I'll give you an example, my old business partner - after a lot of slaps in the face and chronic dermatitis - moved into a company and did better than the other guys like him, with their permanent contracts, right away. In two months he had already been promoted.

Consequently, sacrifice is seen as a central value as well. Francesco described raising large sums of investment in a short time and devoting all his time to a start-up which, after approximately one year of life, has a few employees but he is still not drawing a pay check: "I preferred to invest the funds raised in the company, the first person to receive a pay check was the first intern (...) then, you know, I prefer to get new energies, new brains, rather than anything else... *then there are the taxes, I would rather not pay my own salary*".

However, Francesco's view is not shared by all innovators. For Marc, for example, regulation and labour conflicts are somehow part of an innovation game seen in the Schumpeterian sense as a driver of social and economic change:

> the collaborative economy, *which is a very trendy model*, is questionable if what it does is generate precarious jobs (...) but what needs to change is the regulation... and the industry cannot remain rigid or it will die... look at Airbnb, big hotel chains are investing in holiday rentals to compete with Airbnb (...) or delivery, maybe these companies are not profitable, the challenge will be when the workers are unionised and costs go up and the two-euro delivery in 29 minutes Glovo promises you is no longer feasible. So, automation of deliveries with robots, autonomous cars or drones, that may be the future of delivery.... I don't know, but regulation and the market may not allow them in the future. And if workers unite and fight for their rights, which I think is really fair because these are their rights, working conditions might change and Glovo's economic model might not work. And then they'll have to reinvent themselves or die... I think it's a fantastic cycle that has to keep happening, because innovation is made up of cycles like that, right? Innovate, grow, die...

Innovation and change thus mean different things to the various young people interviewed, just as the start-up concept has no single meaning. Angelo, 29, a Sicily native, moved to Milan in 2010 to study for an MA in marketing and communication. Angelo has recently been working on an innovative start-up, although he tells me has been self-employed since a very early age:

> I have been working since I was 18 years old as a freelance web designer (...) when I enrolled in the MA I already knew that I wanted to be an entrepreneur, to do something on my own. When I started the MA, I had already begun to turn my business into something more structured and over time I created a brand, a small company with some staff, we started developing websites... then I began to launch a couple of start-ups as personal projects, one was in journalism, another was a sort of social network, you know, it was beginning to be fashionable and this eco-system was emerging... and we Italians at that time were famous on the international start-up scene for launching social networks *that did not make a euro...*

When commenting on the newspaper articles employed as visual stimuli during the conversation (see Chapter 1) Angelo, like many other respondents, agreed that the impact of the entrepreneurship rhetoric on young people was making itself felt, feeding their interest in start-ups but also their confusion about what it concretely means to do business, according to the (different) meanings they attribute to it. According to Marc:

> today it is very fashionable to be an entrepreneur, the word is much nicer than *empresario*,[4] it has a more modern, nicer feel to it, but we are all *empresarios* and we all suffer when an *empresario* suffers and entrepreneurs have to be aware of what it means to do this, the economic insecurity, personal insecurity and all the things that happen on that roller coaster that is the first phase of doing business.

The word "fashion" is recurrent in the interviews, as is the term "bubble" to which Pau, among others, refers:

> When we entered the labour market, there wasn't this mania for start-ups, this idea that everyone makes millions with start-ups. We all started with ordinary jobs. But now I see that many more young people leave university and that there are start-ups everywhere and everyone is making

[4] In Spanish, the two terms *emprendedor* and *empresario* are sometimes used as synonyms, and sometimes to distinguish better established entrepreneurs from those operating in contexts of greater risk and uncertainty.

a living with an app. But this is a bubble problem. It is a bubble. They have no idea what it means to start a business.

Almost all innovators interviewed distanced themselves from the start-up rhetoric. In this regard, Angelo is keen to underline the difference between "doing business", which he identifies with the business which developed out of his freelance work, and "doing start-ups":

I see the risk that a little bubble is brewing, that's what the start-up world is today, that is, people who think that launching a start-up means doing business, and it doesn't ... they are feeding into a wrong system made up of people who do things without thinking. There are people who think that all you need is an idea, call it start-up, look for funding, and get two years' salary, with money obtained from a venture capital fund, or from a business angel... this feeds a wrong system and wrong beliefs in young people, it's like university, which is, in some cases, a refuge protecting people from facing up to real life, and then the labour market and all the hardships in it (...) that's what I see. I personally am a member, now, of some start-ups, *very few fortunately*... with young people who have exactly this approach. (...) all the arguments that began during the economic crisis that a secure job no longer exists, that you have to be free, and so on, generated a change in people's mindset, this is happening and it's there, young people are starting to believe in it (...) but whether they are really aware of what it means to do business, I don't think so. I: *you said that launching a start-up is not the same as doing business, what did you mean by that?* A: I'll explain right away. An entrepreneur sets up in business by working on it and imagining it as the company of his life, with no expiry date (...) he doesn't envisage selling it (...) a start-upper creates a start-up with the idea of selling it within 5 years, even within 3 years, that's not doing business (...) and he doesn't want to sell it to develop it further, I mean, there is healthy selling when you say: alright, I get bought up by a bigger company so my tiny company, my little startup, will develop and expand faster ... that's not the goal. The goal is: I'll make a few million and go on holiday. I'm generalising of course, it's not 100%, it's 98% of the examples I came across in the south Italy, Rome, Milan (...) I: *what about your start-up?* A: it was set up with this objective, to be sold. It's no coincidence that we have investors whose purpose is exactly this, they would still force us to sell it, it's in the shareholders' agreements that within a certain number of years they are authorised, even without our permission, to find an advisor who can put the company up for sale and find a buyer...

What is referred to in the jargon as the *exit* is apparently a priority strategy for both investors and start-uppers in line with a financialised "jackpot economy logic" (Luise, 2019, p. 67). The "thoughtlessness" Angelo mentions comes across at least partially in the younger interviewees, among whom it is also worth noting a climate in which start-ups can emerge "a bit as a joke, a bit as a game (...) then we applied to the call for tenders and we won" (Giulia, 26). Still, in cases such as these respondents once again distance themselves from start-up rhetoric. Giulia, for example, says that "the word start-up brings me out in hives a bit, in the sense that anything is a start-up now, it's a bit overused as a term, you know... one of those radical chic terms that are very popular here in Milan". Alessandra, who is 26 years old and worked on a caregivers' platform with some fellow university students with no big initial expectations, detects a great distance between start-up rhetoric and her own experience:

> the *start-up stuff* always makes me a bit sick, because I think we are talking about it in a way... I mean it would be better to talk about companies... start-ups are being mythologised a bit, that is, you are working on a project that you believe in and that you think will develop well and provide good returns... and give you some personal satisfaction. I don't feel like I'm doing anything particularly extraordinary... maybe because for me it's... normal?

In general, as the stories that follow show, the start-up rhetoric is often perceived as simplistic and belittling, as compared to strategies that are actually complex in meaning and reflect attempts by these young people not only to build stable working careers coherent with their needs and aspirations but also to change their living conditions.

4.3.2 *"A Life Project"*

Young people's ability to pursue their ambitions has been profoundly undercut by the major economic and labour market changes of recent decades. Difficulties getting into the job market, widespread employment instability and increasing uncertainty have undermined their ability to dream of, or plan and build, a future for themselves (De Leonardis & Deriu, 2012; Nico & Caetano, 2021; Sennett, 2001). The fact that, as we shall see, most of the young people interviewed expressed a sense of planning through entrepreneurship is, therefore, anything but trivial and reflects how the young adults interviewed are redefining entrepreneurship.

At the time of the interview 34-year-old Adelina from Barcelona had founded an innovative e-commerce business with a friend of hers. Her story is similar to Marc's. She studied business administration and management at a private university in Barcelona, studied for an MBA after graduation and worked for six years in Dubai as a consultant. Then she studied for an MBA at Harvard University, briefly worked in South America for a large company and then again in Dubai. However, the reasons behind her decision to go into business differed from Marc's:

> … then I realised that my life was… not a disaster, but… I was working really too hard, it was really a life project that I didn't want (…) I was working from 9am to 10pm, every day, it was normal, and I was also lucky, there were projects you worked on from 9am to midnight every day, no weekends. I was earning a lot of money, but my life was a disaster….

Adelina was confident about her project and working on a business idea she was passionate about and in which she saw good market potential, but she stressed that the whole project was first and foremost the outcome of a "life choice". The same was true of Paula, also 34, a graduate in business administration, with several years of work experience in a multinational company in Barcelona and two young children. In the interview, she stressed her disagreement with the idea of enterprise as a product to be sold and explained what this project meant to her:

> …a good friend of mine created a start-up which imitated an app in the United States which didn't exist in Europe. After a year and a half she sold it for several million… she was very lucky, but that's not what I want to tell you. After a year she hated it, she was fed up with it, she couldn't stand the sight of it anymore, she didn't like that sector… in my case, this is a life project. I didn't like my lifestyle, I wanted to change my life, do something I like and am passionate about. I also have children and I want to be able to balance the two things, that's what I'm looking for and that's something priceless. I: *how do you reconcile this by doing business?* A: first of all, it's a question of hours and dependence on commuting, I had no flexibility, I had several bosses above me and a company policy that imposed on you… you were expected to work from Monday to Friday, so a certain regularity…. you could ask for flexibility, but first you had

to ask for it and they had to give it to you... the flexibility you have as an entrepreneur is another matter. (...) then you also end up doing many things that you don't... if your boss is in the office, you can't leave. It's not written down, but it's implicit...

For Giulia too—26 and mother of a small child—being an entrepreneur is an opportunity for a better work-life balance, albeit in different circumstances. A history graduate, Giulia's work life was fragmented and precarious when entered the labour market. She thus appeared to be motivated both by low job expectations—i.e. a lack of stable employment alternatives with protection and benefits for working mothers—and a desire to do something she loved and can fit around her care commitments. We met in Milan in a coworking space with a nursery:

certainly, with a baby the project requires a lot of hard work, if I couldn't work here next to the nursery, at a cost absolutely on a par with, if not lower than, a normal nursery, I certainly couldn't do it, because who would look after my baby? My alternative was to work with no guarantees and, in any case, after six months [of maternity leave] with any company I would have to go back to work. This way I can work part-time, part-time is not always guaranteed at firms, and raise my child (...) I want a job that allows me to see my children grow up.

The entrepreneurship choice cannot, overall, be simplified to economic motives or a Californian ideology. Livia is a 27-year-old woman from the south of Italy who first came to Milan to study for a BSc in economics at a private university (with neoliberal economic affinities) which, from her point of view, "tends to give you pre-packaged dreams, and you get into your head that if you do finance you do this, if you do marketing you do this... and you convince yourself that this is your dream, this is what you want, and you don't have to think". Driven by "insane working hours" and dissatisfaction with working conditions, but also encouraged by the uncertainties of employment and a desire for self-fulfilment, she developed an entrepreneurship project with some friends.

Except for Giulia, however, it should be noted that this dissatisfaction with working conditions generally went hand in hand in this group of interviewees with great confidence in their ability to easily get back into the labour market in the event of failure: "I worked in consultancy for a long time, many of my friends and my husband also work in this area, I could easily find a job (...) in a situation like the current one, I could find a job as a consultant in less than a month" (Adelina). It is worth stressing that context is a key component here. The expectations and strategies of the young interviewees were strongly influenced by opportunities and shortcomings in the local labour market.

The reasons behind business creation may also be related to politics. 35-year-old, Barcelona-born Jaume graduated with a BSc in telecommunications engineering in his hometown before moving to Germany for 12 years, first completing an MSc in information technology and then working at a large company. Jaume rejected start-up vocabulary and claimed that his project was best described as a cooperativist experience and a life project in line with his socio-political values:

> I realised that the kind of life I was leading was not coherent with my approach to life. I was working in a purely capitalist company, working for the benefit of investors... and after several years of pondering, I decided this was not the direction I wanted to go, I didn't want to devote that much of my life to pursuing goals that don't really fit my view of the world. Then I came back to Barcelona and started looking for alternative forums, people or communities or organisations with a different approach to economics and life (…) this project interests me because it is a non-profit social project, sustainability is one of its main values. (..) I was really looking for a way to invest my time in a project that is interesting from a sustainability and social point of view, something solidarity-based, non-profit, but capable of making money, because you can't live off air.

While this emerged from one case only, other studies have also highlighted that political ideas and social change concerns can be additional motives for (social) entrepreneurship (Jarrodi et al., 2019). Moreover, as we have seen, Barcelona's government has invested significant resources, both symbolic and material, in providing space and opportunities for new ways of conceiving entrepreneurship, i.e. as a way of promoting social and solidarity-based local economies and cultures.

Contrary to the meaning attributed to their decisions to set up a business, the idea of a quasi-radical change in mindset affecting the very young would seem to prevail among these interviewees. As they see it, young people nowadays are more inclined to appreciate, and take serious consideration of, entrepreneurship as a viable option. Adelina commented as follows on the article claiming that young people increasingly prefer entrepreneurship over office work, for example:

I totally agree [with the article]. My brother is 24 and can't wait to set up his own company. I saw this during the MBA too. I graduated in 2012 and, for many years, the typical MBA options were a job in investment banking or consultancy. People didn't want to do that. I mean, it was a bit like, not exactly for losers, but you were not cool saying: I'm going to a bank, you looked very boring and like "what few ideas you have". I mean, people wanted to go to Facebook, Zinga's or things like that... but there were a lot of people already launching their own companies (...) I think the mindset has changed a lot. And working for a large company is no longer seen as cool.

For Jaume, young people are attracted to entrepreneurship as a reaction to a hostile business and work environment, leveraged to their advantage by financial markets:

I think these articles serve interests that are not those of young people. They try to reinforce the image that being an entrepreneur is positive and that it is a good thing and try to hide or mask the fact that, for the vast majority of young people, being an entrepreneur or self-employed is a necessity. I also have a sceptical view of the rise of startups, in the sense that, as I said before, many have a go and then sell up. I think people don't really get the true meaning of start-up. In theory a start-up is when you find a problem you want to solve, but today many people do it for financial reasons just to sell it.

Experiences tend not to be generalised, then, and youth entrepreneurship is seen as the result of a change in young people's attitudes and preferences, mostly in response to social changes and external constraints.

4.3.3 A Strategic and Meaningful Step

A lack of difficulty entering the labour market coexists with widespread dissatisfaction with working conditions and hours among many interviewees. Raffaele is a 29-year-old engineer:

after graduation, I joined my father's company, but four months later I decided to leave, to use my university degree (...) it went quite well because at the first interview I was hired by a multinational company in the metal mechanics sector (...) for five years I worked for this company, they gave me a permanent contract, and I was a technical officer for my first two years, then I was promoted to the commercial department.

One day, a long-standing friend of his told him about a project he had in mind. They both saw a market opportunity in the idea and decided to join forces on it. Seeing an opportunity was an important factor in this case, but it was not the only reason Raffaele decided to resign from his job:

> I suffered a lot from what I call "corporate slavery", I mean especially when the company was bought up by an American multinational… you have to keep within certain tracks, certain rules that get very oppressive. It almost felt like being in the army. It's true, you're paid, whatever you want… but in my experience… that is, I've always seen my father [working for himself as an entrepreneur]… I found certain things hard… I: *what do you mean by "oppressive rules"*? R: well, first, my salary wasn't good enough for what I was doing… it wasn't low, about 1,600 Euros, it was average… but my duties probably deserved something more, and my level wasn't director level, I wasn't an office manager, I was head of a department… so it was still quite low level, and I had, for example, to notify the firm if I did overtime, and was sometimes even denied overtime, even if there was work to be done… so what does that mean? Working at home. There was also a lot of hierarchy, if your superior said something, even if it was nonsense, you had to do it.

This interview excerpt exemplifies the way in which differentiated drives sometimes intertwine, driving people to leave their jobs and set up in business. On the one hand, the importance of primary socialisation to entrepreneurship within the family is an important factor and, on the other, a local labour market which can be alienating even for highly qualified young people due to wage levels, a hierarchical and authoritarian management style, having constantly and unsuccessfully to negotiate one's rights, i.e. overtime, and the need for promotion for better income and status. All these are considered unmodifiable in a local economy made up of many small firms with paternalistic management styles:

> I: *did you look for work in other companies?* R: well, consider that in other companies I would have found those aspects all too familiar, like those of my father's company, which would have been a problem for me. Perhaps the only thing that might have changed my mind was a doubling of my salary, but that would have been utopian! Maybe in other countries it can be done, but in Italy it is more difficult. (Raffaele)

The structural weaknesses of the Italian labour market emerge more explicitly as factors behind entrepreneurial choices in Giulia's case (a 26-year-old history graduate) for whom enterprise was a personal reinvention strategy, following disappointing experiences in the labour market, made up mainly of small internships:

> these disappointing work experiences were kind of... if things had gone well I would have said: but who's making me do it? That was the determining factor for me. And of course, if my husband had been in a precarious job, or if was impossible to live on his salary alone, I would have given up the idea. That was also a determining factor... that is, the absence of an urgent need to bring home a salary.

The importance of conjugal support reflects the significance of family support in general (and in familistic welfare regimes), in both moral and, potentially, financial terms. It gave interviewees "at least a minimum of back covered (...) maybe you don't need anything, but just in case..." (Dario, 29, Milan). Family also played an important part in Pasquale's story of a highly unusual business project.

Pasquale is a 32-year-old humanities graduate working freelance for several years making very special objects which we will describe here as small paintings to protect his anonymity. When I met him he was working on high-tech product development as part of a team of under 35s and, at the same time, at a fast-food restaurant on a permanent part-time contract. Although he was over-qualified for this latter he never questioned it during the interview and valued it as an "easy job" providing him with a secure, stable income, freeing him of money worries and enabling him to follow his passions:

> it's a part-time job, so it gives me time to do my own thing (...) when I was freelance before I was always alone at my desk, like a spider, painting (...) I hope never to quit my part-time job (...) it doesn't take up too much time, it's well paid, it's open-ended (...) job status matters and it doesn't, in the sense that I personally don't care because I don't equate my value with my job, first of all, and secondly because I get value from what I do outside work (...) consider that if you work full-time as a manager your pay is low for the hours you do... there's a lot of responsibility, the overtime is unpaid, I mean... you have random hours and it's one thing to work 3 hours at night, it's another thing to work... on Saturdays, from 9pm to 5.30am... *it's all OK* but if I can I prefer not to... a life like that

> doesn't leave room for much else (...) I'm trying to set up my life to do what I want, to be free and happy, maybe with a few money problems.

Then he adds: "of course, the premise is that I have a home, so I don't have to pay rent and it's easier to say this...". Housing is indeed a crucial family resource that Pasquale employs strategically, like his part-time job, for what he sees as a meaningful life. While it should be noted that this plays out against a backdrop of full-time work viewed as taking too much away and not giving much back, Pasquale's high-tech product development work is something he is passionate about. And this is how he describes what it means to him:

> Start-upper is a word people use to feed their egos often: I'm a start-upper, that's cool. I don't like it (...) it's a kind of contemporary culture term, like, you're cool if you are a start-upper, but I'm not interested in these things. Mine is a project, even if it is a start-up in the end, maybe we will be start-uppers, but I refuse to define myself in this way.

Our interviewees' motives are thus generally plural, tend to escape static categorisation and reflect a more general tendency for the pursuit of a better work-life balance among young people (Spanò, 2019). This also emerges from young people working in ordinary entrepreneurship, despite the partially different circumstances shaping this.

4.4 "I See It as Something Normal": Ordinary Young People's Needs and Aspirations

> I do this project and I see it as something normal, not in the sense of normal as in a job for life... but in a way automatically... but the interview with you and... now I have been invited to go to a school to do a talk, a few words to some high school kids working on a project, a project to be taken seriously, for real... it's as if we entrepreneurs really have something to contribute and it's important that people want to be entrepreneurs... (Montserrat, 25, Barcelona)

If the accounts of some of the innovators interviewed are imbued with a Schumpeterian ethos, the bulk of the ordinary young people interviewed saw what they were doing as "normal". This ordinariness takes shape within a context characterised by a number of constraints, but from which young people also draw strategically useful information and both material (Chapter 5) and symbolic resources.

Before looking into these experiences in greater depth, it is worth briefly examining some background information on this sample of thirteen respondents. It is gender-balanced, with lower education levels than the innovator sample. The majority had high-school diplomas while one left after middle school and some were graduates. A few were self-employed in graphic design, illustration and photography. Other projects were in the handicrafts, food service and trade sectors. Some of those interviewed were working on developing new products for sale in the field of cosmetics, for example. As we will see, in these cases entrepreneurship decisions were shaped by a more explicit and sharp tension between need and opportunity.

31-year-old Azar was born in Milan to migrant parents. When I met her, she was enthusiastically engaged in the initial stages of a business project which she immediately noted had been inspired by a strong desire for autonomy and entrepreneurship, before describing the circumstances in greater detail:

> the year I got my diploma, I was lucky enough to find work immediately at a chemical company. I worked there for three and a half years, doing a bit of everything, including photocopying, very simple things. It was a highly specialised company and there weren't many growth opportunities for me, because I'm not an engineer nor anything. So I looked for and found work elsewhere, in a Chinese toy company in Milan, and worked there for about five years on commercial stuff like sales, trade fairs and so on. The company was small and there wasn't much chance of growth there either, so I moved to Emilia Romagna where I found a job as company export manager and stayed there for four and a half years. The company … was quite … not big but medium-sized … 150/180 employees, totally Italian. I would say that at a certain point I realised that the problem was not that there were no career openings for me but that the company wasn't mine.

Azar was keen to point out more than once in the interview that she "was always very lucky", mainly because of the ease with which she managed to get into the labour market (unlike her husband), and also because her last job was "very good", well paid and permanent, before continuing:

> what happened was that we had been bought up, because the company was doing very well, the owners decided to make some good money, millions and millions of euros, they sold to an investment fund and a lot of things changed. I decided that I no longer wanted my life to be ruled by things like that, I mean beyond anyone's control. Then when you join a fund, things change a lot, because whilst before the human aspect is important, afterwards it remains important because you still have to work with people, but in the end it is numbers that count most.

She then went on to speak of her "malaise" at the company:

> I wanted to travel for work, that was my dream, it came true, but it was a hell of a dream. If you travel for work in the end you are alone, you don't see as much of the city as you might think, it's tiring, you're doing it for someone else's company, it all started to weigh on me, I felt a need to stay at home, to say *I'm at home*, to cook, clean... I wasn't doing anything anymore (...) I started this company because I had a personal need, a physical, psychophysical need. If it doesn't work out, I have a CV, in a year and a half or two I'll start looking for a new job, but this is something I really had to get out of my system.

In such cases, entrepreneurship is the result of young people's re-elaboration of their experiences in the labour market, including difficulties bound up with overly long working hours, a need for a better work-life balance, mental and physical health issues and, above all, pursuit of a career and what young people see as a meaningful life path.

4.4.1 Building a Meaningful Life Journey

In other cases the preference for self-employment and entrepreneurship was more explicitly adaptive and attributed by interviewees mainly to job insecurity and a significant reduction in the opportunity cost of doing business, a perception resulting from a re-elaboration of young interviewees' labour market experiences: decreasing job security and the protection associated with permanent employment, increasing work-loads and responsibilities in hierarchical organisation and low personal autonomy. For 29-year-old Veronica "it's a bit like a rented house: when the rent is cheap, you pay the rent, when rent is rising, then you buy a house; it's exactly the same".

Veronica opened a small shop where she makes and sells an artisan food product. I interviewed her in her shop during production hours, a few hours in the day when the shop closes while she is in the workshop making her product. She does everything herself, right through from relations with suppliers to production and direct sale, and she told me that she has neither moral nor material support from anyone in her family: "I am completely on my own, without any help… what the hell do I know… throwing out the rubbish, just a stupid example. (…) the hardest thing is that the whole burden is on me, because it's not just the work, I also have the kids, my husband to think of".

Veronica was just 29, but had worked longer hours than any of the others. She dropped out of school at the age of 14 to start work, acquiring the craft skills she later decided to use to set up her business. She was strongly motivated by her need for a reasonable income and working conditions, but also by a desire for freedom and gratification. She expressed great satisfaction and pride in being the *owner* of her own workshop: "[the alternative was] going to work for someone else, being underpaid, working as much as twelve hours a day with no results, because you still… need satisfaction! Now I make something, I sell it, I see joy in people [who taste my product]". Veronica described not having a good relationship with her parents and her whole family had tried to discourage her from opening her shop, which turned out to be much harder than expected. Along with the difficulties, she described her satisfaction at succeeding in setting up her business. Overall, the opportunity to experiment with working on her own, of bringing an important project to fruition, but also her need for gratification and social recognition were all significant elements in a decision which was not simply a matter of the absence of alternatives per se, though it was certainly shaped by a lack of adequate alternatives to the expectations around working conditions, deemed quantitatively and qualitatively unsatisfactory.

For these interviewees, entrepreneurship decisions would seem to have been influenced by a perceived reduction in the opportunity cost of doing business, which encompassed people such as Anne. Just 25 years old, Anne was about to graduate with a political science BA in Milan, having come to Italy in 2011 from central Africa:

> …now I'm doing an MA in resource management, I haven't finished it yet, I still have my thesis to do… at a certain point I realised how difficult it is to get into the job market, being young and especially as a foreigner,

> which makes things more difficult. So I decided to do something, to earn some money too. I did a six-month internship but there was no chance of getting a job after that. Then I saw this call for applications from the municipality, I applied and got in… I: *can't you see many job opportunities even after completing your MA?* R: well, I couldn't find a regular job. I did internships which ended with the internship itself, there was no chance of a job contract, and *we all know how things work here*.

That "we all know how things work here" confirms that the crisis and all the insecurity which went with it are also sometimes a structural element in young people's lives and taken for granted as such (Colombo et al., 2018), prompting "a sort of active resignation" (p. 63). In this case, it interlocks with real and perceived labour market discrimination based on skin colour, in Anne's case, or physical disability, in Letitia's case. I met 29-year-old Letitia in her recently opened Barcelona shop selling handmade goods which she mostly makes herself:

> I studied paper and book conservation here in Barcelona, then I did an MA in England (…) I spent a few years abroad, studying and working… in the end I decided to come back to Barcelona because I like living here better, with my family, friends… I missed it. When I finished my MA I started looking for a job, in book and paper conservation, in archives, museums, I found a few things… but nothing much, I decided to move back to England because I had a job there and so on, but I wanted to live here… so I came back to Barcelona again, kept looking for work, I got a few scholarships at some archives, but nothing for more than six months… so I started considering any job at all, shop assistant, secretary, whatever, but nothing came up… well, in my case, I also faced a lot of discrimination in interviews, because of my problem, and they would tell me: no, we can't have you working with the public, you can't do this …. and well, you know, there's a lot of ignorance. So, in the end, I came up with the idea of creating something on my own.

Under these circumstances, for Letitia entrepreneurship was a way of creating her own stability:

> I probably wouldn't have started this project if I'd had a stable job. The job in England was quite stable, but it was in England. I mean, on one hand it's okay… because every day is a struggle here to get customers, to sell things, but in the long run I think I've got more stability here than the jobs you get today offer you (…) there is no stability in paid work either. I

think that doing what I've always wanted to do I'll find stability when my business goes well. For me, this is more stable than going to work every day knowing that next month I won't have a job.

Entrepreneurship seems to be reinterpreted here as a means with which to embark on a self-built stable and meaningful employment path. 29-year-old Luca, who I met in Milan, provided further insights in this regard. Luca's father was a small businessman who had been discouraging his son from taking over a struggling family business for years, persuading him to continue with his education. Luca thus enrolled at university to study law but soon realised that it was not for him, left and ran the family business, having decided to convert production with the help of municipal incentives. He seemed to see no valid alternatives to this and was driven by a strong desire for self-fulfilment whose only outlet he saw in business:

I: *Don't you think there might be stimulating job opportunities in the labour market?* R: No, because... if you start searching for a path, not a job, then yes. You take a path and keep following it... I never took a path in that sense. I knew that my future was to continue with this activity or to take a path. I: *what do you mean by path, can you give me some examples?* A: for instance, a legal path... you study, then you do well for yourself, you do a good job, well paid, over time you progress...

It is noteworthy that Luca equates entrepreneurship with university. Both university and enterprise are, in fact, seen by him as strategies with which to construct a coherent and meaningful life "path", as opposed to the fragmentation of "odd jobs":

I waited tables here and there (...) nothing very satisfying, I mean... I didn't see the point, if I had needed to I would have done thousands of odd jobs, definitely (...) but working in Piazza Cavour [a square in Milan], to be honest... for how I see work, I don't want to. I: *what do you think work should be?* R: Well, a passion... it's not just about earning money (...) for example this company, the idea of my father's company being rethought, Dad seeing his dream come true and me trying to promote a traditional local material and knowhow... tradition, that's certainly more stimulating.

This questions the meanings young people attach to work, i.e. what they aspire to achieve through work, which are increasingly complex and not simply a matter of instrumental aspects such as wages. This representation also takes shape from an awareness of the existence of a production context made up of companies just like his father's: "why would I work for someone else when I can work in my own company? It didn't make sense…". Luca's was ultimately a choice designed to build a path which made "sense" to him, including as a strategy to preserve his social status.

4.4.2 *"You Must Do It All Yourself and Make the Most of It"*

Further reasons behind the shift to self-employment-entrepreneurship are linked to changing employment relationships, particularly in certain sectors, and the "active resignation" mentioned previously. Fabiola is a case in point. At 28 and as a former student at one of the municipal vocational schools running entrepreneurship support projects in Milan (Chapter 3):

> I was already contemplating self-employment before I enrolled in the school (…) also because I had already been in paid employment… then I got into an internship after I finished school. In the end it lasted nearly a year. The internship was not offered by the school, I found it by myself and this was a step I wanted to take, I felt it was necessary before throwing myself into self-employment (…) I believe that in qualitative, personal, creative and many other terms, self-employment is really a rewarding choice, especially in these times, both economically and in terms of quality of life and personal satisfaction.

However, she sees this choice as virtually forced given the circumstances:

> Paid employment hardly exists anymore now in our sector. So many young people work in studios but self-employed, I think it's unacceptable, there are internships that are extended beyond acceptable timeframes, I worked a few months without a contract, it's today's reality. The only difference if you're self-employed is that the money goes into your bank account, if you're an employee you see the money when your boss is in the mood (…) in our field it's getting tough.

Indeed, the use of short-term employment contracts has increased in recent years in these sectors, together with bogus self-employment, low wages and long hours (Murgia et al., 2016). 25-year-old Montserrat, who lives in Barcelona with her family, recounted experiences which speak volumes in this sense. She had a university degree and a passion for photography that she is trying to turn into her main occupation:

> I looked for a job in September, all the offers were: you have to be an expert in photography, post-production, programming, you have to have years of experience and the salary is minimal, and you think: mmm, no (...) now I have a problem with a company because they used to have a trainee who worked 5 hours a day, Monday to Friday, and earned 400 euros a month, working on something like the final photos for 40 products. Well, I did 12 products in one day while she did about 40 in a month. I charged them something like 20 euro per hour, for 7/8 hours. They said that for this price they couldn't pay me, but I won't work for 400 euros either. This company and I don't understand each other because I want to work with them and they want to work with me, but I'm not going to sell myself so cheaply. This is what happens.

Exposure to work insecurity would seem to be higher among young people carrying out traditional entrepreneurship projects than for most of the innovators, and it also seems to have a more explicit influence on the entrepreneurship choice in a specific socio-cultural context. Indeed, the ordinary young people interviewed tended to take living in a context that requires them to accept greater individual responsibility and cope individually with uncertainty for granted. For example, commenting on the newspaper articles, Veronica expressed the opinion that if there is a greater interest among young people in entrepreneurship "it's a good thing, so at least we are a bit more... [think a bit about the word to use] protected? ... or rather, we protect ourselves, because otherwise we can no longer move forward". Similarly, Montserrat argued:

> I saw my aunt... who is the only entrepreneur in the family. She always said there were too many problems, too many concerns, too many responsibilities... now she has a bigger company, but I always said: no, I don't want this for me, I want a monthly pay check. But *the mindset has changed now* (...) and nobody gives you anything, *you have to get on with it yourself and make the most of it*.

Uncertainty, the problems and specific dynamics of local labour markets and production structures, the focus on individual responsibility, and so on, is not only taken for granted, but it also seems to be viewed pragmatically by young people in both Milan and Barcelona and with a watchful eye on the opportunities to "be taken advantage of", in Letitia's words, to try to embark on new and potentially more fertile paths. It is in this context that entrepreneurial and self-management skills acquire meaning and value:

> I have a 15-year-old cousin. Now at school he takes entrepreneurship lessons... he learns how to do entrepreneurial projects... this is important because you have to be ready whatever you end up doing. I think economics, management, how to implement a business idea should be compulsory at school. Well, now I suppose this is starting, but it wasn't there in my day. (Letitia)

> We have to be creative, we have to be up-to-date, we have to keep working on public relations, we have to cultivate old and new customers, we have to be empathic... all this has to be worked on and acknowledged (...) if multinationals want us, it is certainly because they recognise that we are far ahead of paid employees, who don't have to deal with the outside world for God knows how many years... (Fabiola)

Such skills seem to constitute a set of symbolic resources which young people draw on to build a positive self-representation and justify the choices they make too. These are choices which, as we have seen, are influenced by a variety of factors. On the one hand, they were used by the young people interviewed to rework their labour market experiences and implement strategies managed in a pragmatic and targeted manner (Katz, 2004). This interlocked with locally situated demands for subjectivity and the pursuit of self-expression through work, social status and upward social mobility, and symbolic remuneration that are increasingly significant to young people coping with the growing individualisation permeating contemporary society (Murgia et al., 2016; Nico & Caetano, 2021; Spanò, 2019) and which pre-existing public policies aim to support.

The next chapter will explore the way these pressures relate to the local context and MESPs in greater depth, and provide important resources that young people draw on, albeit in diverse ways and with differentiated outcomes, as part of attempts to build careers consistent with their dreams, attitudes and aspirations.

References

Aldrich, H. E. (2005). Entrepreneurship. In N. J. Smelser & R. Swedberg (Eds.), *The handbook of economic sociology* (pp. 451–477). Princeton University Press.

Colombo, E., Leonini, L., & Rebughini, P. (2018). A generational attitude: Young adults facing the economic crisis in Milan. *Journal of Modern Italian Studies, 23*(1), 61–74.

European Commission. (2016). *The state of European cities 2016*. Publications Office of the European Union.

De Leonardis, O., & Deriu, M. (2012). Introduzione. La capacità di aspirare come ponte tra quotidiano e future. In O. De Leonardis & M. Deriu (Eds.), *Il Futuro nel Quotidiano. Studi Sociologici sulla Capacità di Aspirare* (pp. XI–XXII). Egea.

De Luigi, N. (2007). *I confini mobili della giovinezza. Esperienze, orientamenti e strategie giovanili nelle società locali*, Franco Angeli.

Eurostat. (2022). *Statistics Explained article on employment in detail - quarterly statistics*, https://ec.europa.eu/eurostat/statistics-explained/index.php?title=Employment_in_detail_-_quarterly_statistics#Developments_by_type_of_activity (accessed 01/07/2023).

Evans, K. (2002). Taking Control of their Lives? Agency in Young Adult Transitions in England and the New Germany, *Journal of Youth Studies*, *5*(3), 245–269.

Jacobs, J. (1970). *The Economy of Cities*, Penguin.

Katz, C. (2004). *Growing up global. Economic restructuring and children's everyday lives*. University of Minnesota Press.

Jarrodi, H., Byrne, J., & Bureau, S. (2019). A political ideology lens on social entrepreneurship motivations. *Entrepreneurship and Regional Development, 31*(7–8), 583–604.

Luise, V. (2019). *Le Forme dell'Innovazione nell'Ideologia Californiana: le Retoriche, i Modelli e le Trasformazioni nell'Economia Startup*. Egea.

Manzo, C., & Pais, I. (2017). I Fondatori di Startup in Italia tra Agency e Struttura. *Quaderni di Sociologia* (73), 9–28.

Murgia, A., Maestripieri, L., & Armano, E. (2016). The precariousness of knowledge workers: Hybridisation, Self-employment and subjectification. *Work Organisation, Labour and Globalisation, 10*(2), 1–9.

Nico, M., & Caetano, A. (2021). *Structure and agency in young people's lives*. Routledge.

OECD/European Commission. (2019). *The Missing Entrepreneurs 2019*. OECD Publishing.

Pinson, G., & Morel Journel, C. (2017). *Debating the neoliberal city*. Routledge.

Rossi, U. (2017). *Cities in global capitalism*. Polity Press.

Schumpeter, J. A. (1947). The creative response in economic history. *The Journal of Economic History, 7*(2), 149–159.

Sennett, R. (2001). *L'uomo flessibile. Le conseguenze del nuovo capitalismo sulla vita personale.* Feltrinelli.

Sheehan, M., & Namara, A. M. (2015). *Business start-ups and youth self-employment: A policy literature review synthesis report* (STYLE Working Papers, WP7.1). CROME. University of Brighton.

Spanò, A. (2019). Giovani e lavoro: cambiamenti dei significati del lavoro in tempo di crisi. *Sociologia del lavoro, 154*(2), 203–222.

Sternberg, C. (2023). *Neoliberal urban governance. Spaces, culture and discourses in Buenos Aires and Chicago.* Palgrave Macmillan.

CHAPTER 5

Differentiated Inclusion

Abstract This chapter sheds light on the ambivalence inherent in inclusiveness as a guiding principle of entrepreneurship support policies and the differences (re)produced in the MESP field in the wake of inclusiveness. The aim is to try to capture the way MESPs interlock with pre-existing socio-economic and cultural inequalities and enquire into the ability to redistribute resources and opportunities between young people. It highlights the main dynamics of "differentiated inclusion" generated, especially along the "innovative" and "ordinary" youth dividing line, by the simultaneous interaction of differentiated and differentiating policy instruments and pre-existing inequalities. In doing so, this chapter critically questions the assumptions implicit to inclusive entrepreneurship policies implementations and emerging contradictions starting from the idea of a definitive democratisation of entrepreneurship.

Keywords Inclusive entrepreneurship · Democratisation of entrepreneurship · Inequalities · Barcelona · Milan · Start-up ideology · Individualisation

"Write your own future", "no dream comes true until you wake up and go to work", or the Pablo Picasso quote: "inspiration exists, but it has to find you working": these are some of the inspirational slogans on the

M. Dodaro, *Unpacking the 'Start-up City'*,
https://doi.org/10.1007/978-3-031-50212-5_5

facade of one of Barcelona Activa's incubators. Not only are these slogans present in the start-up world (Luise, 2019) but they also resonate more generally with the central principle underlying individualisation processes, namely that everyone is to be expected to take responsibility for their lives and occupational "projects", a view which has also become a widely taken-for-granted assumption.

Most of the people interviewed, including the young people receiving business support, agreed that what really matters in entrepreneurship success is commitment, perseverance, individual skills, or *execution*, in current parlance. This latter is a matter of the value accorded team expertise, business design and planning in enterprise development, as well as the process of fleshing out the project idea. The performative power of this discourse is meaningful, as we shall see, in either magnifying the role individuals play in the success or failure of their project ideas, or concealing the extent to which young people's entrepreneurial planning is shaped by the tools and resources available to them. The "garage myth" notwithstanding, awareness of the importance of context and public action would appear to be stronger now. Entrepreneurial paths are locally embedded and, arguably, the emphasis on "ecosystems", "start-up cities" and so on also plays a part in bringing the importance of the collective resources facilitating business development into the open. Although individual ability to take advantage of locally available opportunities counts equally for the young people interviewed.

As we have seen, ensuring these opportunities are open and accessible even to those with the most limited resources is the explicit goal of cities' inclusive entrepreneurship support policies. To this end, cities have set up differentiated tools aimed at diverse targets. This differentiation reflects on business projects, entrepreneurs' profiles and their personal biographies, the latter being characterised, as Chapter 4 explored, by a similar complexity and pluralism of business project meanings, i.e. what they aspire to achieve, but also by significant differentiation in the circumstances contributing to people's decisions to become "entrepreneurs". As we will see below, the available resources also differ, as do the risks involved in taking this step. Admittedly, such policies provide support tools in this context whose importance is in direct inverse proportion to beneficiaries' material, social and symbolic resources. However, the differences (re)produced in the MESP field in the wake of inclusiveness also deserve attention if we are to be able to critically question the assumptions implicit to their concrete implementation and emerging contradictions.

My intention is to try to capture the way municipal entrepreneurship support policies (MESPs) interlock with pre-existing socio-economic and cultural inequalities and enquire into the ability to redistribute resources and opportunities between young people. The starting point for this reflection concerns one of the main assumptions underlying inclusive entrepreneurship policies and current start-ups rhetoric: the idea of a definitive democratisation of entrepreneurship.

5.1 The Democratisation of Entrepreneurship Promise

> The revolution is that with 20 euros you can buy a domain, set up an app and launch a project. This democratises the chance to do business and opens it up to all young people to do it with ... well, we had some savings and we put in 40,000 euros, which is a lot of money, but there are probably people who start up their businesses with 2/3 thousand euros and that's all it takes to try the idea out. (Marc, young entrepreneur, Barcelona)

The idea that doing business is a cheaper alternative to employment than in the past is widespread among interviewees, but certain differences between policy stakeholders and beneficiaries, and within this latter group according to the specific set of constraints and opportunities shaping their actions, are also visible. As we will see later, for many young interviewees, and probably for many young people experiencing economic uncertainty and vulnerability risks to various extents, the forty thousand euros mentioned by Marc is often either unachievable or subject to specific conditions, using up all one's savings or risking a bank loan, when credit is an option and no other funding opportunities are available. However, the availability of personal financial resources is generally seen as the least crucial form of capital for business start-ups, in both Barcelona and Milan:

> Economic resources are something of a myth. It is true that they are important, but they tend to be especially important when projects require high investment. What is more, the economic issue arises when an enterprise wants to grow further. It is a bit of a myth, young people's projects do not usually require very large investment. (Entrepreneurship Directorate, BA)

Several dynamics have contributed to generalising from certain specific cases. Firstly, the increasing availability of ad hoc funds for both innovative (e.g. venture capital) and conventional (e.g. microcredit and government incentives, often promoted under inclusive entrepreneurship programmes) business projects. Secondly, an increase in business opportunities related to the tertiarisation of the economy. Indeed, young self-employed people in the EU are more likely to work in less capital-intensive sectors with low barriers to entry, such as many service sector spheres (OECD/European Commission, 2019). But it is, above all, the availability of financial instruments with which to support innovation that has contributed most to the idea of a democratisation of entrepreneurship, since this encompasses the most innovative and rewarding forms of entrepreneurship which require significant funding to grow but are accessible independently of the availability of large family capital. It is worth emphasising that in both contexts the tendency to take family support for granted in the nascent stages of a business, either in the form of economic aid (however limited as compared to the capital accessed by innovative start-ups) or through broader support (e.g. living at home) is common. In these terms, Milan and Barcelona are influenced by a more general Mediterranean welfare model (Esping-Andersen, 1990) and youth transition regime (Walther, 2006), in which the family historically plays a central role in social protection and the transition to adulthood.

The idea that structural inequality factors, and the availability of economic capital in particular, are declining in importance tends to be accompanied by an emphasis on individual ability, willpower, determination and a good business idea:

> Funding is a fairly common concern for all projects, but if a project has a face and eyes, I mean it is a good project, well developed, that really has potential, feasibility, if there is a team of proponents, but if there is just one person it is the same… however, if the person or people behind it are a good team… it is a matter of going and knocking on doors and funding will come. It is true that not all projects end up getting funded, for one reason or another. But if it is a good project, it is a matter of time, patience and perseverance… (Consultant, BA)

Even where the relevance of other factors, i.e. qualifications or family support, is recognised:

> [the people who contact the microcredit service include] few graduates, but those who come here, and are selected, if they have a good family network they do very well. Those who are more fragile, more alone, I admit that most of those coming here are of this second type… well, some of these succeed and some don't… and this is all a matter of determination, luck and a lot of ability and a willingness to put yourself to the test. (Microcredit Manager, Milan)

It follows that support services, aimed mainly at developing and improving business plans, and more generally at enhancing entrepreneurial knowledge, skills and attitudes, are seen as essential to inclusive youth entrepreneurship:

> In our opinion, entrepreneurship is a skill that can be learned. If you want to start up a business, you have to learn everything to do with that business, like a dentist training to become a dentist. You have to know your market, know who your competitors are, know why your price is this and not that, where to buy your supplies, where to get the money. These are things you don't know if you have never set up a business… but they are essential. Often people come to our advisory team with decisions already taken, the wrong decisions, and of course sometimes we can't help, because they have already rented a place that is not suitable for what they want to do. For example, renting a children's clothing shop in a neighbourhood where only elderly people live… sometimes they come with these decisions. (Entrepreneurship Directorate, BA)

The general view is that entrepreneurial skills can be learned, and this tends to be seen as important to ensuring that the self-employment career option is open to everyone and increasing the chance of success, in the current labour market context:

> It is usually said that "entrepreneurs are born, not made". Actually, we have somewhat turned this way of thinking on its head and adopted "entrepreneurs are born and made" as our slogan… because there actually are specific characteristics and personal predispositions which are also learnt in the family… because living in a family where parents are entrepreneurs obviously helps. Others have a vocation and entrepreneurship comes naturally to such people. But, with the evolution of the labour market, and therefore changes to employment contracts, the idea of setting up one's own business and, therefore, entering the labour market as a self-employed person or an entrepreneur has become a further option,

> I wouldn't say easier, but... worth considering, to broaden one's labour market opportunities. (Consultant, Milan)

This has two main implications. On the one hand, soft supports to entrepreneurship like these can offset certain differences in cultural capital among young beneficiaries, including by reducing the risks involved and, as we saw in Chapter 3, fostering greater awareness of the concrete opportunities and risks faced (including discouraging entrepreneurship). The fact that these inherently act only downstream of the circumstances in which the decision to set up in business and in what form is taken, however, tends to greatly reduce their impact on a broader redistribution of risks and opportunities among young people. I will examine this point later. The second implication concerns the way in which the emphasis on individual skills blurs the macro-social factors behind projects' success or failure. Indeed, the latter are often attributed by young people themselves—especially by men with innovative projects—to personal causes, as exemplified by these interview excerpts in which young people share their thoughts on the dynamics underlying their career success (Angelo) or the difficulties putting their projects into practice (Domenico):

> I associate everything with the fact that as a child I always played with Lego, so I developed this desire to build and create, which is the phase that interests me most, that is, the thing that most stimulates me is to create something from scratch and see it grow, develop and generate something, generate value. (Angelo, young entrepreneur, Milan)

> ...here there is a skill deficit. I: *what are you lacking in your view*? R: certainly a bit of entrepreneurial initiative ... even maybe, okay, let's make the product before signing the contract we're waiting for. Because we know how much it costs... but before investing this money... we want to be sure the contract is there. (Domenico, young entrepreneur, Milan)

Although the risk of failure inherent in innovative start-ups is generally acknowledged and the socio-economic risks bound up with it for socio-economically vulnerable young people have been taken into account in the public sector in both contexts (Chapter 3), the tendency within MESPs is to reiterate the images implicit in the positive hegemonic discourse on entrepreneurship. In particular, this includes the idea of entrepreneurship as always positive and desocialised, the assumption that the "entrepreneurial ecosystem" or "start-up city" is capable of inclusively offering the same opportunities to all without more general social, economic and cultural factors being taken into account (Essers et al., 2017). This sees young people as a homogeneous group facing similar constraints (e.g. difficulties entering the labour market, precariousness, over-education) and, in line with ongoing individualisation processes, in control of their own destiny.

5.2 Differentiated and Differentiating Policy Instruments

The principle of inclusiveness has, as we observed in previous chapters, been incorporated into urban agendas in both Milan and Barcelona and translated into differentiated entrepreneurship support tools, reflecting urban economy diversity and different concrete entrepreneurship practices: from the most *innovative* (e.g. high-tech start-ups) to the more *ordinary* (e.g. traditional service sector businesses). The emphasis on innovation, particularly technological innovation, that has accompanied start-up city development in several countries has often ended up overshadowing the latter. Yet, traditional businesses have significant importance within MESPs which, as we have seen, reflect material and discursive local investment in inclusive entrepreneurship support policies. This is the result not only of cities acknowledging and reproducing the inclusiveness principle that important steering institutions such as the OECD and the European Union are encouraging them to incorporate into their programmes, but also—and this is one of the book's main arguments—of bottom-up pressures driven by both a widespread entrepreneurial and business culture and a demand for autonomy, self-fulfilment and subjectivity from some younger people and not just innovators, but all the young people interviewed, in line with more general individualisation processes.

However, the inclusiveness principle does not automatically translate into a real redistribution of youth opportunities. The normative character of the concept of inclusion suggests that this is a predictable outcome, but it actually isn't. There are two main risks inherent in the normative concept of inclusion. The first is underestimating the complexity of the motives behind some young people's decision to consider entrepreneurship (Chapter 4) and reducing the problem to the obstacles in the way of such decisions. Appreciating the multiplicity of the underlying problems might shift the focus from how to make entrepreneurship viable for all to how to widen the range of available solutions for young people (by addressing the complex relationship between young people and the labour market). The second risk is contributing to individualising the blame for failure, or the merit for success, obscuring the social nature of the differences produced and reproduced within MESPs. Differentiated policy instrument do, in fact, have differentiating effects, albeit in a circle generated by the interaction between various instruments and pre-existing inequalities.

5.2.1 *The Social and Cultural Dimensions of Differentiated Inclusion*

The young participants in this research differed in various respects, most notably in socio-biographical terms, such as educational attainment and gender. As we have seen, most of the innovators interviewed were men and this reflects a wider gender gap in the start-up universe and its imaginary. The Schumpeterian entrepreneur is typically identified with traits traditionally associated with masculinity (innovation's creative destructiveness, the desire for success, power, wealth), and this has contributed to constructing an image of entrepreneurship consistent with these characteristics, however biased it might be (Bruni et al., 2004). Gender differences are also partly related to educational backgrounds and in particular to lower numbers of women studying STEM subjects at university (OECD/European Commission, 2019). Education, as we saw in Chapter 4, is crucial to entrepreneur-innovators' lives (Manzo & Pais, 2017; OECD/European Commission, 2019). First of all, STEM studies seem to have given the young people interviewed greater employment confidence, as they are considered to be in demand on the labour market, albeit with some of the limitations already discussed:

> Engineering is a qualification that is still in demand on the labour market, but it is also a qualification that doesn't pay well in salary terms, at least in Italy...So, I know that I can do it...you also need to have self-confidence. I know that if anything goes wrong, I could do a few job interviews and sooner or later I think I'd find a job. (Raffaele, young entrepreneur, Milan)

The majority of Barcelona Activa's applicants are generally graduates (72% in 2018; Barcelona Activa, 2019). No overall data is available for Milan but projects supported by incubators or innovation-oriented programmes tend to be almost exclusively led by graduates in both cities according to interviewees. By contrast, a significant share of the young people setting up ordinary or traditional businesses also had low or medium–low educational qualifications. Certain programmes, such as entrepreneurial microcredit in Milan, almost exclusively involve young people with lower levels of education facing greater difficulties entering the labour market, especially in stable employment.

As far as transition to the labour market is concerned, the education to work transition for young respondents with high levels of human capital tends to be smooth, i.e. relatively obstacle-free. Furthermore, work experience would seem to contribute to building an effective resource base that young people can mobilise when setting up in business. The opportunity to work for a few years in a company doing qualified work would seem to enable them to acquire greater knowledge and confidence. Previous work experience is a very important resource that young people draw on to build strong social networks and acquire skills of immediate use in business, even if they are not directly entrepreneurial. This was true of Pau who was able to experiment with developing an internal entrepreneurial project (i.e. *intrapreneurship*) at his Barcelona firm which he coordinated for a few years (see Chapter 4).

However, a widespread dissatisfaction with working conditions was tangible across the board in the interviews and closely bound up with the entrepreneurship decision. In particular, the women interviewed stressed the difficulties involved in balancing work with other spheres of life, especially social and care commitments. For these women, start-ups were "life projects" (Chapter 4), opportunities for a more flexible career and better work-life balance. Of course, this was not true of all the women interviewed. Self-employment-entrepreneurship, especially in traditional sectors, often involves longer working hours (Sheehan & Namara, 2015) which, in a context in which care responsibilities and housework tend to fall mainly on women, makes achieving balance difficult. This was true of Veronica:

> I cried more when I set up this business than when I got married. I could hardly drag myself out of bed in the morning, for me it was... I was so scared (...) so many people were down on the idea... because with two

> children you know, it's a bit more difficult. My husband started saying that I was never at home any more, what are we to do with the children, what we're not doing ... a week after I opened, I was fed up ... then my mother stepped in: "ok, are you sure you want to do this? Well, you know I'll never help you out". It's just that ... you know, not to have even just a little support... that's really bad. (Veronica, young entrepreneur, Milan)

In this case, choosing to set up in business to improve her economic condition and, at the same time, meet a need for self-fulfilment (see Chapter 4) implied not only a major effort in various spheres, but also, for Veronica, feeling hugely blamed by her family and not being able to count on the support of her relatives, support which most of the interviewees did have, to a greater or lesser extent. Family plays a very important role in both contexts. Firstly, it provides material and moral support and, secondly, it supplies fundamentally important socialisation to entrepreneurship by transmitting a heritage of family experiences from childhood onwards that is also consistent with a cultural model (entrepreneurial culture) deeply rooted in the wider local context.

After family, social capital also plays a very important role, i.e. the network of relationships and contacts that young people can draw on and is a further dividing line between young innovators and other young people. Indeed, all the innovative project developers interviewed were working in teams of at least two, either friends or fellow students. In the technology start-up world, teamwork and a high level of expertise are considered key to persuading potential investors to fund the business project. Both teams and cultural capital levels are not, however, seen as inconsistent with the democratisation of entrepreneurship by virtue of the desocialised, and thus purely meritocratic, associations of this form of capital and thus this method of selection:

> access is democratised in the sense that anyone can compete, anyone can enter. Key to retaining a competitive advantage in the technological world is, I believe, the team, the people you have, and this cannot be copied. It makes human capital more important than in any other industry. This is fundamentally different, I think. And then funding capacity. If you have a good team you can raise more money, if you raise more money you'll definitely win. (Marc, young entrepreneur, Barcelona)

By contrast, young people with ordinary entrepreneurial projects generally set them up on their own, as the characteristics of local enterprises show (most have zero employees, see Chapter 3). This is also confirmed by interviews with sector staff:

> Most of the time it's just one person... we have many projects run by a single person (...) it's often purely self-employment, i.e. the idea of creating your own work, I do it myself and I take all the responsibility and risk involved, I make the necessary investment, I look for the funding I need, I do whatever it takes, but for myself. (Consultant, BA)

Going into business alone entails a different workload, stress and responsibility: "the trouble was setting up as a sole trader. At the beginning it was very difficult... it was hard to do it alone. It is different when you can swap views with another person" (Luca, young entrepreneur, Milan); "the main problem is that you sometimes feel very lonely" (Montserrat, young entrepreneur, Barcelona). Carlo (young entrepreneur-innovator, Milan) noted that "many are afraid to start something that is bigger than themselves. I, honestly, couldn't do it alone".

Moreover, young people setting up traditional businesses sometimes take greater individual risks, as the next section shows.

5.2.2 *The Higher the Business Risk, the Lower the Individual Risk-Taking?*

Other significant differences emerged with regard to individual risk-taking and responsibility, aspects historically assumed to be inherent to entrepreneurship (Pirone, 2023) and pivotal entrepreneurial subjectivity models. Self-entrepreneurs are active, responsible individuals whose fate depends on their own decisions and willingness to take individual responsibility for the risk these entail. Innovative entrepreneurship is considered especially risky due to the higher uncertainty inherent to innovation processes and innovators are, by definition, those taking the greatest risks. However, if risks and responsibilities are examined at the individual rather than enterprise level, they seem to have a greater impact on young respondents engaged in "ordinary" business projects. First of all, it should be remembered that, at the enterprise level, too, there are various legal forms which entail different risks and responsibilities. In particular, there are two forms of "business liability": limited and unlimited. In a nutshell, limited liability means that a firm's owners are not individually liable, legally speaking, for any debts it may incur, while in other cases owners are personally liable for debts with their own assets. Limited liability thus provides greater protection against risk but also, in the case of innovative start-ups, the opportunity to access specific funding opportunities.

The financial instruments available to young people vary by type of enterprise. While "ordinary" businesses usually turn to the traditional credit market, "innovators" usually target primarily venture capital. This also explains why programmes such as microcredit cannot provide much help to "innovators", as the manager of the microcredit service in Milan explained:

> ninety-nine per cent of what we do is in the crafts and services sector (…) none of the people I've met so far in my work with the municipality's social innovation incubator need microcredit, because they get funding from the finance sector, which is throwing money into innovation. Also, these tend to be businesses that turn a profit in… two or three years. So I find it difficult to convince these people to use this instrument… they don't need it, they have other forms of funding (…) innovation doesn't fit in, because its time-to-market and profitability times are too long.

Just as the financial instruments available vary, so do the opportunities to reduce (or externalise) risks, as well as the opportunities to access large amounts of capital. Indeed, start-ups' main sources of funding are venture capital, angel investors, forms of equity crowdfunding, i.e. forms of funding that do not involve repayment and in which the high risk involved in innovative start-ups is taken on by one or more investors in exchange for shares. The innovative start-uppers interviewed often aspired to access this type of funding. This allowed respondents both to avoid exposure to banks and to circumvent the constraints potentially arising from difficulties accessing credit:

> I: …*why didn't you go to the bank?* R: It's a matter of risk. Do you want to take such a huge risk for a business idea? No, to be honest. If there is a capital fund that gives you…firstly, these funds usually finance ten start-ups and, if they are lucky, two of them do well and make a profit…so, we know that the death rate is extremely high, so… taking risks like that… we don't want to and neither does anyone else here. (Fabio, young entrepreneur, Milan)

A reluctance to take risks and expose oneself to economic risk is sometimes seen by some of the start-uppers themselves as proof of both a purely instrumental value in the start-up world—i.e. a means of enrichment in financialised capitalism—and the weakness of enterprise projects (as it denotes a lack of belief by start-uppers themselves in the economic potential of their projects). This distances the representation of start-uppers from the ideal of the "good entrepreneur" taking economic and business risks. According to Angelo, for example:

> entrepreneurs believe in their projects and are willing to invest their own money in it right away, that take a personal risk. Start-uppers actually presume to set up in business without risking even a single euro out of their own money but, right from the start, with their sheet of paper and idea, they want to go and look for money from others to get started. (Angelo, young entrepreneur, Milan)

Besides, start-ups are a type of enterprise that often requires high capitalisation and, as Luise (2019) has explained, several agents invest in start-ups with a view to increasing their financial value and then converting them into profits for sale in a varying period of time, i.e. *exit*. The funding to be obtained through these channels is considerable (six million euros in Marc's case, Chapter 4) and such that municipal economic incentives (when present, as in the case of Milan's support programme for social start-ups) come across as almost insignificant in comparison: "nothing" in the words of Francesco (24, Milan), "a drop in the ocean" for Angelo (29, Milan). From this point of view, "innovators" and "ordinary" young entrepreneurs seem a world apart:

> I'm not an expert on this, but my feeling is that they have easier access to funds in the innovation field. For example, yesterday I met a young woman who had managed to get hold of 250,000 euros for her digital platform in just one year and it hasn't earned a single cent yet. I thought 'wow'! The ease with which she obtained these funds surprised me, she was surprised as well because her boyfriend couldn't get 30,000 euros for his café, she was also surprised he needed some guarantees…I said to her: well, you are in the world of innovation, he is in the normal world of credit access! (Microcredit Manager, Milan)

The "normal world of credit access" is the context in which the practices of young interviewees setting up their ordinary businesses tend to be situated. In these cases a combination of savings and subsidised loans is the main source of funds. For example, Veronica (29, Milan) obtained around 20,000 Euros in microcredit (i.e. a loan covered by a public guarantee fund), less than half of the investment she needed to open her shop:

> The microcredit was 20,000 euros, I had to find the rest...I can assure you that it was hard (...) the investment was much higher... where did this money come from? My pockets are now empty I can tell you ...it went badly also because my brother-in-law promised me some money but then gave me much less. So I had to take those few savings...basically, I took them away from my children, because I had opened a bank account to save some money for them and I had to take those savings with the hope of putting them back.

In Milan, the specificities of the measures these young people had access to must also be considered. The key, explicit priorities of programmes such as microcredit are precisely beneficiary financial inclusion, i.e. guaranteeing access to credit for vulnerable individuals with no access to ordinary channels because they lack the required personal guarantees. Hybrid supports, such as municipal resources for businesses in the city outskirts, provide non-repayable funds and credit (microcredit) which involve some financial risks, as we saw in Chapter 3:

> ... the state gives us nothing without getting its own return, not a single euro, because if the project goes well, only 25,000 euros of the 100,000 they give us does not need to be paid back. We pay 20% VAT, so they give us 5000 euros, which they get back in the first years in tax.... I mean, they're not losing anything, they recover all this in a few years basically. It's not giving away anything. If you close, on the other hand, *you* have to pay the debt. (Karim, young entrepreneur, Milan)

In other cases, ordinary young people have only their savings and the help of their families to rely on. However, the main concern tends overall to be less the risk of losing these savings—a risk they take into account—than not being able to develop their projects, build their future working lives. This is the main issue at stake:

> I'm not worried about losing my money. Because it's not... it's money invested, for me, it's not money lost. I mean, most of the things I have

> here are mine. Yes, the rent and everything... but if I were doing other things, I would also be spending money. No, my fear is not being able to make a living from this, not being able to be independent and make my own money from it, earning a living. (Letitia, young entrepreneur, Barcelona)

Overall, young interviewees setting up traditional businesses are subject to greater constraints than their peers in the innovation field. They also have much less time, since their businesses must be able to generate revenue right away for two main reasons. Firstly, their savings are more limited. Secondly, even if the loans they agree to include a transitional period (in microcredit, for example, this period is one year), their income must soon be sufficient to cover both the loan and their business costs.

The young people interviewed thus responded to the challenges of individualisation but their levels of economic, cultural and social capital varied and they had less time available to them. Some succeeded, but with more of a struggle and varying rewards.

5.2.3 *Reward Expectations and Alternatives*

In the context outlined here, a further differentiation element worthy of attention is the distance between what is at stake for, or expected of, interviewees involved in innovative start-ups as compared to the others. In general, innovative start-ups are high-tech companies whose mortality risks are high—although they do not necessarily translate into equally high individual risks, as we have seen—but their growth potential is significant:

> If you get ten million euros and you can start over... you're starting at another level... I wouldn't set up a single company, I'd invest in several companies. I would have a portfolio of companies... more than just one. If you come out with 500,000 euros instead of ten million... well, probably what I would like to do is to start up another company and sell it for 50 million ... in the end, what I would like to do is generate the maximum possible value, through something that motivates me, which is setting up companies, innovating, generating jobs... (Marc, young entrepreneur, Barcelona)

In general, young innovators have great ambitions and high expectations of financial returns from what they do but also personal success:

> Employees' ambitions are growth and perhaps promotion and thus more money than before. We have more than one, I mean, it's our vision, let's call it a vision, it's not just about earning more but also about making a success of your business. So, see your business grow, improve and… be more and more successful in today's world. (Carlo, young entrepreneur, Milan)

These "employees' ambitions" echo those of young respondents in *ordinary* business. In fact, the economic and personal success legitimately pursued by young innovators contrasts significantly with the expectations of those setting up in business to create their own jobs and salaries, as emerged in the excerpt from the interview with Letitia quoted in the previous section, and a professional identity:

> It was nice to be able to create my own workplace, it is nice when the phone is already ringing at 8:30 in the morning… it is nice because it means that you've managed to create something and make yourself independent, make something of yourself… be appreciated for what you do. (Carmelo, young entrepreneur, Milan)

> Very few businesses set up with microcredit exceed the threshold… survive. They survive but microcredit does not make people rich, they can't even be said to earn that much. Even after four or five years people are doing well, they are earning, they have improved and stabilised their standard of living, but they're not rich. Very few enterprises have managed to make the changes of scale required to make them entrepreneurs who can really do serious business. (Microcredit Manager, Milan)

At the same time, the alternatives (and, thus again the risks, in the event of failure) vary. As we have seen, those with a technical-scientific background have highly positive perceptions of the labour market alternatives in the event of failure. This is not the case where it is labour market difficulties which played a significant role in the decision to set up in business, due to a lack less of alternatives tout court than of viable and better alternatives to self-employment:

> Traditional business suffered, yes, but were there people who quit traditional business to get a job? No, because there were no jobs either. Then, of course, when employment alternatives do begin to appear, we will see if people… if their businesses are more profitable than the job offers they get, and I tell you the answer is no. Because we have a general problem with

> salaries in this country. I'm talking mainly about medium-high level posts and first hires, in particular, not people who have been working for 20/25 years probably with good salaries because they were well paid before too. (Entrepreneurship Manager, BA Private Partner)

The risks, responsibilities and potential rewards vary then. However, one point raised in the previous chapter should be stressed: regardless of these differences and the various circumstances shaping young people's decision to become entrepreneurs, they all are passionate about their projects. A positive attitude, a desire to get things done and make a success of themselves, is not a prerogative of "innovators", whatever the additional resources available to them (see also MacDonald & Coffield, 1991).

5.2.4 *Local Public Action and Youth Coping Strategies*

Barcelona and Milan are two cities that, as we saw in previous chapters, do not simply provide a backdrop to young people's entrepreneurship-based coping strategies, but are both influenced by them and actively involved in providing material, social and symbolic resources. The presence of young people from other countries among those supported reflects the economic and social dynamism discussed in Chapter 2. In 2016, 30% of those presenting entrepreneurial projects to Barcelona Activa were born abroad (16% of these were from the EU) most of whom lived in Barcelona municipality or province (BA, 2019). It is difficult to determine how many of these came to Barcelona specifically to set up in business. Only two of those interviewed for this research were born abroad and in both cases their mobility was closely bound up with their entrepreneurial projects (an innovative start-up and a restaurant):

> We looked at Barcelona because we thought it would be a good place to set up in. (…) it has a young population, it's a cosmopolitan city, it's not very big, it's small, so… we saw that there are a lot of creative restaurants and clubs here, different things from other countries. Then we saw that there was space for our kind of business. Here there are spaces for thematic, gourmet things…. I could compare it with the United States, New York, for example. And then there are lots of foreigners looking for our type of cuisine because they are nostalgic for their own countries, and curious people. When we came in June, we did the training session in Barcelona Activa and we went around the neighbourhoods and felt that there are

> many different places, different from those you see in other cities. (Linda, young entrepreneur from Latin America, Barcelona)

In Milan, the presence among the interviewees of several young people—all "innovators"—from the south and other regions of northern Italy choosing Milan as the ideal context for their businesses was significant:

> In my opinion, if you want to set up a tech company in Italy, Milan is definitely the liveliest city to do it in, both for the services you have access to, and for the user base there of people who are perhaps more accustomed to using online services. (Luigi, young entrepreneur, Milan)

This is mainly to be explained by the overall features of the city and an "ecosystem" ranging "from the funding you find, to the networks of start-ups, incubators, accelerators, the local authorities, coworking spaces…" (Antonello, young entrepreneur, Milan) that make everything easier. On the other hand, the municipal economic incentives provided by some programmes to support innovative start-ups in Milan (Chapter 2) do not seem to play a decisive role in the decision to set up in business in general (or even specifically in Milan). They are, in fact, actually often considered of marginal importance, given innovative start-ups' high capitalisation needs. Soft supports are considered important, especially in Barcelona, due to Barcelona Activa's high reputational capital. However, they seem overall to be an extra resource to be used to strengthen one's networks and project within a framework of strategies well-designed to make the most of all available opportunities:

> Barcelona Activa was our incubator, and the truth is that we used it quite a lot because it is a reference point in the entrepreneurial world and the fact of being accepted by Barcelona Activa… sends out a message that your project makes sense, if they give you a space it is because they believe that your company has a certain potential. Then, the environment of BA is very entrepreneurial, you make lots of contacts, people who are at the same stage of development as you, and this can support you because BA's structures give you some support. It's true that in our case we already knew, through the MBA, we had a lot of contacts, including with investors directly… but being in BA gave us an office in a place where there was a very important breeding ground for innovation and start-ups. (Marc, young entrepreneur, Barcelona)

In the case of young interviewees setting up ordinary businesses, on the other hand, municipal support is often decisive. This is particularly evident in Milan, where economic incentives played a key role in moving this group of interviewees from intention to action. These resources enabled participants to reduce some of the business risks (when non-repayable funds were available) but above all, they gave them access to the economic resources needed to start up their projects through subsidised credit and/or public guarantee funds (microcredit). This support was used to strengthen entrepreneurial projects and sometimes back up the legitimacy of applicants' decisions both to themselves and their families. This was true of Azar who pooled her savings and the non-repayable funds she accessed through the municipal call for business start-ups in city outskirts:

> maybe I would have set it up in any case, but not immediately… I didn't have the money to set up a company. I would have had to apply for a conventional loan, which would have required personal guarantees that I didn't have (…) without winning the call for tenders I would have had a much harder time even getting… moral support… at home… (Azar, Milan)

> I lost my job, and I was getting by on temp agency contracts, three months here, six months there, then I saw this municipal call and (…) I had this abandoned workshop that was my dad's, and I wanted to put it to good use… and (…) everything was perfect… the street was ok [it fell within the city outskirts area targeted by the call], the idea fitted … it was perfect! (Lorenzo, Milan)

But soft support can also be crucial to the decision to set an entrepreneurship project in motion since, whatever the more complex reasons, MESPs provide extra incentives and resources to put these into practice:

> I knew I had this passion, but that was all… then I found out about the Barcelona Activa programme [Idees amb Futur]. It was great because they helped me a lot with all topics. (…) a friend and I went to a fair…. Job Barcelona. We went with the idea of finding a job because we were unemployed at the time…. (…) we were about to leave when we saw a Barcelona Activa stand, so I signed up (…) one day they sent me an e-mail informing me of a programme presentation. (Montserrat, Barcelona)

> About three years ago, I had to choose whether to continue working in a studio in Milan, where I was working as a graphic designer, or to change, to get a VAT number (…) fortunately, when I was about to make this decision, this spin-off, opportunity at the school came up and I applied (…) from then on I got a lot of support (…) everything started with this opportunity. (Fabiola, Milan)

Municipal support in some cases can also help to diminish the sense of loneliness those setting up individual enterprise projects can feel. Unlike "innovators" who always work with one or more partners, the other young people interviewed had to make decisions alone and expressed a need for "at least one other person to talk to or exchange views with", to be able to share concerns and decisions with someone. In this sense, Veronica found someone at the microcredit accessory services (coaching) with whom she could share doubts and problems, and get technical information on starting up a business. Montserrat, on the other hand, explained the importance for her of taking part in a course designed to help those attending to manage their emotions and difficulties related to self-employment provided by Barcelona Activa:

> Barcelona Activa helped me a lot. There was also a coaching course and I really liked it because… sometimes this thing of being self-employed… well, if you have doubts or problems… you have no one to say: look, can you help me for a moment? No, you are alone. (…) I also took a course at Barcelona Activa on managing your emotions. I: *sounds interesting*… R: very interesting. Because sometimes you're sad, but you have to work… until you explode. So, you learn to listen to yourself and look at what happens to you, understand that if you are sad… there's nothing wrong with that… there were also many girls, in the group there were 20 female entrepreneurs! I thought I was the only one with this problem… and now we also have a WhatsApp group and we're helping each other out.

This kind of support—a training course designed to help people cope with the emotions and anxieties that come into play when you set up in business—partly reflects the tendency to individualise problems and solutions that underlie MESPs. However, it also provides pragmatic responses to the tensions arising from the need to deal individually with the risks and responsibilities involved in doing business, generating contacts, swapping information and developing mutually supportive practices, perhaps even unintentionally.

Overall municipal support can be a very important resource within young people's more general entrepreneurship-based coping strategies. However, one of the things which has come out of this book is that local public action and youth coping strategies intersect with dynamics that we might call "relational", in Bourdieu's words, insofar as both government and individual action take shape within a broader social, economic and cultural system. The role that cities and MESPs play can thus be viewed in the light of the broader economic, social and cultural changes outlined in previous chapters which: (a) feed both young people's demands for subjectivity and requirements made of them for individual responsibilisation and activation; (b) reduce the opportunity costs involved in doing business or perceptions of it; and (c) contribute to constructing entrepreneurship as a homogeneous reality, a phenomenon that is always positive and, therefore, a desirable as well as concretely viable alternative to paid employment.

5.3 Individualisation: Growing Opportunities, Worsening Inequalities?

> In these years of crisis, we have seen new generations made up of highly competent, highly educated people excluded from the labour market or in precarious jobs. These people are deciding to take their present and future into their own hands, saying: well, let's develop a project. (Consultant, Barcelona Activa)

Walther contended that "individualisation means that new opportunities arise while social inequalities prevail" (2005, p. 116). While the space for experimenting with and bringing life projects more in line with individuals' personal needs to fruition may grow, this increasingly implies making decisions, taking risks and responsibilities with often inadequate safety nets for those who fail. It is a failure that is hardly even contemplated in the collective imaginary of young entrepreneurs and interviewees, whose essential traits have been outlined. Within this framework, we have seen that entrepreneurship's meanings are pluralistic and often varied greatly from one interviewee to another.

In some cases, at the apex of what we might envisage as a "start-up city" pyramid populated by the young people best armed with economic, social and cultural capital, entrepreneurs take the Schumpeterian guise of innovators animated by a will to create, win, succeed (Schumpeter, 1947). In most cases, entrepreneurship is primarily a life project, a way of reconciling work with other spheres of family and social life, of building a meaningful, even stable, life trajectory, despite entrepreneurship being the very epitome of uncertainty. This paradox is only apparent if we consider the circumstances via which young people's strategies take shape and the importance of entrepreneurial culture in their local contexts. Contexts influence young people's strategies and contribute both to shaping the possible options open to them and the availability of both the material and symbolic resources to bring plans to fruition. Moreover, it is only superficially paradoxical, given the broader context of individualisation within which the perception that it is possible to take control of one's own destiny with the resources at one's disposal is spreading (Spanò, 2018). This is a tendency towards self-responsibility that stems directly from the models of individualisation that are informing both public and individual action. In the face of unequal risks and rewards, it should be noted that a positive attitude, determination and aspirations to bring a personal (life and enterprise) project to fruition is not a prerogative of the young people with the best economic, social and cultural capital. The decision to do business is in many cases also an example of the "active resignation" (Colombo et al., 2018) that develops when crisis is internalised as a natural and constant fact, and from the agency of young people expressed in the form of targeted, pragmatic responses to challenging situations in times of profound individualisation.

References

Activa, B. (2019). *Memòria d'activitats 2018*. Barcelona Activa.

Bruni, A., Gherardi, S., & Poggio, B. (2004). Doing gender, doing entrepreneurship: An ethnographic account of intertwined practices. *Gender, Work & Organization, 11*, 406–429.

Colombo, E., Leonini, L., & Rebughini, P. (2018). A Generational attitude: Young adults facing the economic crisis in Milan. *Journal of Modern Italian Studies, 23*(1), 61–74.

Esping-Andersen, G. (1990). *The three worlds of welfare capitalism*. Princeton University Press.

Essers, C., Dey, P., Tedmanson, D., & Verduyn, K. (2017). *Critical perspectives on entrepreneurship. Challenging dominant discourses*. Routledge.

Luise, V. (2019). *Le Forme dell'Innovazione nell'Ideologia Californiana: Le Retoriche, i Modelli e le Trasformazioni nell'Economia Startup*. Egea.

MacDonald, R., & Coffield, F. (1991). *Risky business? Youth and the enterprise culture*. The Falmer Press.

Manzo, C., & Pais, I. (2017). I Fondatori di Startup in Italia tra Agency e Struttura. *Quaderni di Sociologia* (73), 9–28.

OECD/European Commission. (2019). *The Missing Entrepreneurs 2019*. OECD Publishing.

Pirone, F. (2023). Imprenditorialità e società capitalistiche. In Morlicchio, E., Cocorullo, A. (Eds.) *Dieci lezioni di sociologia economica*. Franco Angeli.

Schumpeter, J. A. (1947). The creative response in economic history. *The Journal of Economic History, 7*(2), 149–159.

Sheehan, M., & Namara, A. M. (2015). *Business start-ups and youth self-employment: A policy literature review synthesis report* (STYLE Working Papers, WP7.1). CROME. University of Brighton.

Spanò, A. (2018). *Studiare i giovani nel mondo che cambia*. Franco Angeli.

Walther, A. (2005). Risks and responsibilities? The individualisation of youth transitions and the ambivalence between participation and activation in Europe. *Social Work and Society, 3*(1), 116–127.

Walther, A. (2006). Regimes of youth transitions. Choice, flexibility and security in young people's experiences across different European contexts. *Young, 14*(2), 119–139.

CHAPTER 6

Conclusions

Abstract By addressing the lack of in-depth empirical knowledge of what lies behind the "start-up city" label, and calling the reader attention to the contingent ways the neoliberal entrepreneurship rhetoric is put to work, contested and resignified by local actors, this chapter argues for a multi-scalar and nuanced understanding of municipal entrepreneurship support policies, as well as of urban neoliberalisation. It discusses MESPs' ambivalence by taking the three different but interconnected levels on which youth entrepreneurship practices and policies are situated into account. The first of these is the macro-level of the socio-economic and political-cultural dynamics informing both public and individual action. The second is the meso-level covering the specificities of national and local contexts. By taking young beneficiaries' opinions and the meanings they associate with entrepreneurship seriously, the third is the individual and subjective level. This chapter highlights how the interaction between these levels results in locally embedded macro-processes redefinition.

Keywords Entrepreneurship policies · Youth entrepreneurship · Neoliberal urban governance · Local actors agency · Local embeddedness

European cities are not only a microcosm of macro-phenomena and global processes but also a force field in the Bourdieusian sense of a plural,

M. Dodaro, *Unpacking the 'Start-up City'*,
https://doi.org/10.1007/978-3-031-50212-5_6

incoherent and conflicting domain of interests, attitudes, aspirations—and fears of loss—of status, ideas and representations of the world (Amin & Thrift, 2007; Le Galès, 2002).

Within the limits of this study, mostly stemming from the significant heterogeneity of both urban economies and entrepreneurship policies and practices, this book's aim was to improve our understanding of neoliberalising trends in urban policies and governance by presenting novel knowledge on municipal entrepreneurship support policies (MESPs) focusing on the cities of Barcelona and Milan. In so doing, it has sought to address a current lack of in-depth empirical knowledge of this topic and the reference literature's silence on local actor agency. By applying a combination of neo-Marxian and neo-Weberian interpretative frameworks to the urban political economy and through cultural political economy and sociological analysis, the book has examined what lies behind the "start-up city" label, and the way local actors reproduce, contest and resignify entrepreneurship policies and practices in a highly individualised context. From the starting point of observing MESPs' inconsistency with the monolithic and homogeneous representations conveyed by the discourses, symbols and practices revolving around the economic imaginary of the "start-up city", the book has shed light in particular on MESPs configurations in ways that depend on both overarching dynamics of economic and social change, and on local processes in which certain combinations of interests, representations, values, policy approaches and practices take shape.

The book began by showing that it has been above all its coherence with long-running economic, social and political-cultural developments that has given the start-up economy its tangible grip on cities and policies at various levels. Barcelona Activa—set up as a business incubator over thirty years ago—is vivid proof of this. The "start-up city" developed first of all in the context of the rise of entrepreneurship and the revival of Schumpeterian theses in the 1980s under the aegis of neoliberalism, understood as "a theory of political economic practices which proposes that human well-being can best be advanced by the maximization of entrepreneurial freedoms within an institutional framework characterized by private property rights, individual liberty, free markets and free trade", in which "the role of the state is to create and preserve an institutional framework appropriate to such practices" (Harvey, 2006, p. 145). A Californian ideology imbued with a belief in entrepreneurship, technological determinism and economic liberalism (Luise, 2019) fits into a previously mapped out enterprise culture path typical of the neoliberal ethos and which Du Gay defines as a culture in which "certain enterprising qualities - such as self-reliance, personal responsibility, boldness and a willingness to take risks in the pursuit of goals - are regarded as human virtues and promoted as such" (1996, p. 56). Consistency with other dominant economic imaginaries, such as the knowledge economy (Jessop & Sum, 2010), and the persuasive power of the vague, prescriptive, decontextualised and depoliticised entrepreneurship discourse (Essers et al., 2017), have further contributed to endorsing entrepreneurship as a panacea for all ills (Swedberg, 2000), a highroad to sustained innovation, economic development, employment and social inclusion through processes driven by individuals, small businesses and local governments (Fiorentino, 2018).

The relevance of entrepreneurship to the EU's economic and social development framework has given business creation and self-employment support measures growing legitimacy in many cities and these have been boosted not least by the circulation of European ideas and recommendations in city networks. Entrepreneurship policies and practices also evolve in conjunction with individualisation processes that, on the one hand, steer public action towards approaches and models of intervention geared towards individual responsibility, activation and self-reliance and, on the other, bring in models of socialisation hinging on personal capacities to develop individualised and flexible personal initiatives and professional strategies, adapt to changing circumstances and reorganise one's life primarily to serve such strategies (Castel, 1997, 2004). Models like these additionally enhance the same demand for autonomy and self-fulfilment opportunities, especially among the young, whose available resources vary by socio-biographical background (e.g. class, gender, age, nationality), however, and are always responses to increased social and labour insecurity (Beck & Beck-Gernsheim, 2002; Bifulco, 2017; Walther, 2005). In this sense, entrepreneurship is paradigmatic because it implies models of action and behaviour, and values, that are fully consistent with "individualised forms of existence" (Beck, 2002, p. 182), while concealing the risks inherent in its positive portrayal and youth resourcefulness rhetoric.

In the light of this various scholars (Fiorentino, 2018; Moisio & Rossi, 2020; Pollio, 2020; Rossi & Di Bella, 2017) see the start-up city as revelatory of a political rationality designed to universalise enterprise and market rationale across society, penetrating social actor representations, beliefs, dispositions and behaviours in depth. This interpretation rests on a body of literature on entrepreneurial and neoliberal transformations of urban policies and governance. On this basis, it frames the start-up city on a continuum with Harvey's theories of cities' "entrepreneurial turn" (1989, p. 14), marking their convergence on development models revolving around competitiveness, attractiveness and economic growth. These soon turned into imperatives, thereby strongly influencing the urban agenda in the European context, too (Pradel & Garcia, 2021).

This book has sought to account for these dynamics while not losing sight of local actor room for manoeuvre and the ways they resignify and attempt to turn entrepreneurship policies and practices in other directions. While cities' prominence in entrepreneurship support may provide evidence of the way in which "the late neoliberal city has since ingested and internalized entrepreneurial logics themselves", as Peck (2014, p. 399) puts it, the MESPs analysed here showed a more nuanced picture, developing both at different times and in different ways, depending on local specificities, including institutional legacies, local policy cultures, governance models, the political orientations of local governments and the socio-economic characteristics of the two cities. This same active city role contributes to opening up spaces for some local actors to resignify and sometimes challenge the entrepreneurship paradigm and the start-up economy rhetoric.

Local government agency is sometimes expressed by shifting the focus to alternative economic models, such as the social and solidarity economy (Barcelona), through support for the proximity economy in the outskirts (Milan) and, in both cities, as action in support of the urban independent middle class, to some extent impoverished by the economic and social consequences of globalisation, and by paying special attention to young people. The integration between MESPs and the economic and social fabric of the "everyday city" (Amin & Thrift, 2007) is hardly self-evident, since the start-up economy as an economic and business models would seem to be disembedded from local economies—favouring "their embeddedness in global networks and flows of ideas, discourse, knowledge, technical expertise" and capital (Rossi & Di Bella, 2017, p. 1005)—and detached from the political and cultural dynamics of cities. The "start-up city" thus conceived is in fact also a depoliticised city, in which there is no space in which to question the choice, neutrality, positive character goals and representations underlying entrepreneurship policies and practices.

However, the MESPs' political dimension in Barcelona and Milan was not homogeneous, but divergent and sometimes contradictory, even combining opposing political choices. In Barcelona, the weight of entrepreneurship policies has varied over time according to the political orientation of local governments, leaving room for alternative conceptions of entrepreneurship and, through this, of the economy and society as well. In Milan, the MESPs' political dimension is weaker, reflecting a historically laissez-faire local governance model and the prominence of private initiative, with a less substantial directing public actor role than Barcelona's. Action to deter entrepreneurship rather than promote it, under certain conditions, notably when it conflicts with other policy objectives (such as limiting the risk of exacerbating social vulnerability) is more in line with the pragmatism that characterises Milan's local policy paradigm, however MESPs fulfil this function in Barcelona as well.

Discouraging entrepreneurship under certain conditions highlights the ambivalence of the growing "demand from below" for entrepreneurship support, a demand that is grounded in entrepreneurship's capacity to catalyse expectations of work, self-fulfilment and social recognition, and only in some cases a desire for enrichment or mere adherence to the Californian or enterprise ideology. It was above all the interviews with young beneficiaries which cast light on this aspect, one which is consistent both with ongoing individualisation processes and with a local entrepreneurship culture that goes beyond the neoliberal enterprise ethos. In this regard, many of the stories chronicled in the previous chapters were illustrative of the role that cultural models inherited from families of origin play in young people's experiences and the meanings they attribute to entrepreneurship. These are aspects that, intertwined with the characteristics of the (urban) economy and the labour market and the changes underway in them, further boost the entrepreneurship which MESPs foster.

Support for entrepreneurship is thus also viewed by local governments as a way of supporting the strategies of the segment—mainly young and often highly educated—of the urban population whose response to labour market challenges is entrepreneurship (Pacchi, 2018). The latter is an important but insidious point since these are individualised professional strategies requiring the availability of resources (not only economic, but also interpersonal, cultural), a circumstance that does not take into account inequalities between young people and which interacts with differentiated policy instruments, as we have seen. This differentiation is in part the outcome of inclusive policies designed under the European "inclusive entrepreneurship" policy framework. But it is also premised on the implicit assumption that different people will establish different businesses in economic sector, degree of innovation, reference financial markets and growth potential terms. The heterogeneity of entrepreneurship is often portrayed as natural, and at times as a theoretical problem, related to the absence of a single definition, or methodology, and the related measurement challenges. It is more rarely seen as a phenomenon constantly reproduced through programmes and initiatives attempting to promote entrepreneurship as a viable alternative for all, based on, and reproducing, this differentiation.

MESPs' ambivalence can best be understood by taking the three different but interconnected levels on which youth entrepreneurship practices and policies are situated into account. The first of these is the macro-level of the socio-economic and political-cultural dynamics informing both public and individual action (notably the dissemination of neoliberal regulation models, individualisation processes, financial, economic and labour dynamics and related impoverishment phenomena). The second is the meso-level covering the specificities of national and local contexts, and the third, the individual and subjective levels (motivations, circumstances behind the business decision, inherited cultural models, aspirations and meanings that young people attribute to entrepreneurship). The interaction between these levels results in locally embedded macro-process redefinition.

Both macro-level processes and national and local contexts effectively condition both young people's policy options—which they choose between—and the set of constraints acting on, and resources available to, them and which influence their aspirations and success (Evans, 2002; Nico & Caetano, 2021; Spanò, 2017). National and local contexts are relevant in this respect for a number of reasons. Firstly, the national institutional framework contributes to delineating an unfavourable context for young people in both Italy and Spain with their do-it-yourself state welfare cultures. Both countries can—drawing on the well-known categories elaborated by Esping-Andersen (1990) and Walther (2006)—be defined as providing a sub-protective transition (to adult life) regime in response to young people's residual social rights (e.g. income support, education and housing), the weakness of active policies (including vocational training, counselling, job seeking assistance) and dependency on family of origin. This context influences young people's own coping strategies, the options they consider, their viability, and which options they ultimately choose (Spanò, 2018).

These institutional forces intersect with local labour market dynamics (Migliavacca & Rosina, 2022). While employment trends in both Milan and Barcelona outperform those of their respective national contexts, labour market transformations and the 2008 economic crisis have had a significant impact on entire new generations, even in "stronger" urban contexts. The 2008 crisis had diverse but important repercussions on all European cities. However, its impact on Barcelona and Milan was especially severe, and contributed to a climate of continued structural lack of opportunity: Anne's despondent "we all know how things are here" in the interview reported in Chapter 4. The crisis and perceived socio-economic changes seem to be starting assumptions informing the aspirations, expectations and practices of the young people interviewed (Colombo et al., 2018).

The ambivalence inherent to contemporary European cities is also of note, with their growing inequalities and exclusion processes and, at the same time, their ability to catalyse work, enterprise, education and training opportunities (Cucca & Ranci, 2017; European Commission, 2016; Le Galès, 2002). These are not solely and exclusively a matter of concern for young people from the urban elites but, albeit to different degrees and in different ways, also impact on "ordinary" young people, to borrow Woodman's (2013) definition of young people who are neither the "more excluded" or the "more spectacular" (p. 179). However, some aspects of these job opportunities have remained in the shadows. As we have seen, fewer young people are looking simply for any old job (Migliavacca, 2022). At the same time, a lack of employment per se is often not the main problem in young people's difficulties with the labour market in Barcelona and Milan.

A large body of literature (Bertolini et al., 2022; Blossfeld et al., 2005; Unt et al., 2021) has documented that structural changes in the labour market since the 1980s have disproportionately affected youth employment by increasing non-standard work—temporary, part-time, more or less genuine self-employment—in most EU countries. In some cases, this may help facilitate the labour market inclusion of those facing higher barriers to entry (such as young people or women), enabling them to acquire relevant information, expand their network of contacts and, in general, gain experiences that may prove useful in their careers. The entrepreneurial path itself, as we have documented, is generally taken in adulthood after some working experience has been acquired together with sufficient cultural, social and economic capital. However, it is often dissatisfaction with multiple dimensions of work that contributes to motivating young interviewees' entrepreneurship choices, forcing us to question the nature of youth work even in "strong" contexts. This theme may be an interesting future research direction. Labour market changes have led to progressive impoverishment and a deterioration in working conditions resulting in unstable incomes, precariousness and limited opportunities for professional growth, and sometimes also mental health issues, as evidenced in some of the interviews presented in this book.

The book, and Chapters 4 and 5 in particular, have shown that young people respond in a targeted, pragmatic way to problematic situations through entrepreneurship in a context of individualisation and internalisation of part of the relevant frames of reference, thus exerting a form of situated agency. If we take young people's opinions and the meanings they associate with entrepreneurship seriously, it highlights the way entrepreneurship practices incorporate and reproduce models of subjectivity and society consistent with ongoing individualisation processes, but also that these do not fully fit into the entrepreneurial or neoliberal subjectivity frameworks. However unequal the contexts, young people attribute plural meanings to entrepreneurship which do not automatically overlap only with instrumental motives, such as market opportunities or desires for enrichment (as well as a self-earned wage). Beyond the undoubtedly important instrumental aspects ("you can't live off air", as Jaume said in Chapter 4), the particular salience acquired by expressive values and the need for "symbolic rewards", such as social recognition and other non-monetary forms of gratification (Fumagalli, 2015), should also be considered.

While it is true that the entrepreneurial choices made by young interviewees setting up non-innovative business projects seem to be more explicitly adaptive than that of the "innovators", relying on a more pronounced tension between need- and opportunity-based reasons, and subject to greater constraints, it is also true that the constraints do not seem to override other pressures, meaning that choices cannot be simplified to purely fall-back motives. Entrepreneurship practices reflect a more general pluralisation of the meanings of work, understood as a tool with which to aspire not only to a salary, but also to social recognition, gratification and self-expression, as something to make a living from but not the be all and end all (with other aspects remaining important, hence the demand for better work-life balance, expressed by women in particular). Among the young people interviewed, these meanings, needs and aspirations take the form of pressures for entrepreneurship and lives and careers to which interviewees attribute meaning, sometimes as a response to the fragmentation of odd jobs, or toxic work, which is well paid but leaves no room for anything else, and often openly contrasting with the youth entrepreneurship rhetoric. The latter is contested above all as it is perceived as an attempt to attribute meanings to young people's experiences which they do not identify with.

In this context, policies offer support instruments whose relevance increases in inverse proportion to the material and symbolic supports available to beneficiaries, as we have seen. However, their relevance in this respect has not prevented a deeper analysis of the ambivalence of entrepreneurship support policies, highlighting a number of limitations related, in particular, to differences (in risk and opportunity terms) reproduced in MESPs including in the name of inclusiveness. As we have seen this differentiation is partly bound up with MESPs' very heterogeneity, with their diverse measures and programmes for different targets. On the other hand, it has a structural basis in the diverse characteristics of the young people interviewed, both in past experiences acquired (such as cultural capital, and especially qualifications, and social capital) and ascribed characteristics (including gender, class, race, disability). These characteristics can either strengthen or weaken young people's room for manoeuvre—as much if not more than the availability of economic capital or entrepreneurial skills—which is, it should be stressed, nevertheless, locally embedded (Nico & Caetano, 2021). In this sense, the primary focus on activation and individual responsibility underpinning inclusive entrepreneurship policies—in line with principles inspiring the welfare state reforms of recent decades—risks justifying inequalities, rather than fostering a more equal distribution of opportunities and risks (Bifulco, 2017).

Cities' responses to the ambivalence of inclusive entrepreneurship policies are not always adequate or capable of expanding less the inclusive capacity of specific policy instruments than existing alternatives, in a way that gives young people a plurality of desirable and feasible options.

References

Amin, A., & Thrift, N. (2007). Cultural-economy and cities. *Progress in Human Geography, 31*(2), 143–161.

Beck, U. (2002). *Cos'è la globalizzazione*. Carocci.

Beck, U., & Beck-Gernsheim, E. (2002). *Individualization: Institutionalized individualism and its social and political consequences*. Sage.

Bertolini, S., Borgna, C., & Romanò, S. (2022). *Il lavoro cambia e i giovani che fanno? Tra struttura, aspirazioni e percezioni*. Franco Angeli.

Bifulco, L. (2017). *Social policies and public action*. Routledge.

Blossfeld, H. P., Klijzing, E., Mills, M., & Kurz, K. (Eds.). (2005). *Globalization, uncertainty and youth in society*. Routledge.

Castel, R. (1997). Diseguaglianze e vulnerabilità sociale. *Rassegna Italiana di Sociologia, 38*(1), 41–56.

Castel, R. (2004). *L'insicurezza sociale. Che significa essere protetti?* Einaudi.

Colombo, E., Leonini, L., & Rebughini, P. (2018). A generational attitude: Young adults facing the economic crisis in Milan. *Journal of Modern Italian Studies, 23*(1), 61–74.

Cucca, R., & Ranci, C. (2017). *Unequal cities: The challenge of post-industrial transition in times of austerity*. Routledge.

Du Gay, P. (1996). *Consumption and identity at work*. Sage.

Esping-Andersen, G. (1990). *The three worlds of welfare capitalism*. Princeton University Press.

Essers, C., Dey, P., Tedmanson, D., & Verduyn, K. (2017). *Critical perspectives on entrepreneurship. Challenging dominant discourses*. Routledge.

European Commission. (2016). *The state of European cities 2016*. Publications Office of the European Union.

Evans, K. (2002). Taking control of their lives? Agency in young adult transitions in England and the new Germany. *Journal of Youth Studies, 5*(3), 245–269.

Fiorentino, S. (2018). Re-making urban economic geography start-ups, entrepreneurial support and the makers movement: A critical assessment of policy mobility in Rome. *Geoforum, 93*, 116–119.

Fumagalli, A. (2015). Le trasformazioni del lavoro autonomo tra crisi e precarietà: il lavoro autonomo di III generazione. *Quaderni di ricerca sull'artigianato*, 2, 225–254.

Harvey, D. (1989). From managerialism to entrepreneurialism: The transformation in urban governance in late capitalism. *Series B, Human Geography, 71*(1), 3–17.

Harvey, D. (2006). Neo-liberalism as creative destruction. *Series B, Human Geography, 88*(2), 145–158.

Jessop, B., Sum, N.L. (2010). Cultural political economy: Logics of discovery, epistemic fallacies, the complexity of emergence, and the potential of the cultural turn. *New Political Economy*, *15*(3), 445-451.

Le Galès, P. (2002). *European cities: Social conflicts and governance*. Oxford University Press.
Luise, V. (2019). *Le Forme dell'Innovazione nell'Ideologia Californiana: Le Retoriche, i Modelli e le Trasformazioni nell'Economia Startup*. Egea.
Migliavacca, M. (2022). Quantità o qualità? Le sfide del lavoro per i giovani europei. *Quaderni di Rassegna Sindacale, 1*, 115–120.
Migliavacca, M., & Rosina, A. (2022). Il posto dei giovani, tra presente e futuro. *Social Policies, 1*, 3–14.
Moisio, S., & Rossi, U. (2020). The start-up state: Governing urbanised capitalism. *EPA: Economy and Space, 52*(3), 532–552.
Nico, M., & Caetano, A. (2021). *Structure and agency in young people's lives*. Routledge.
Pacchi, C. (2018). Sharing economy. Makerspaces, co-working spaces, hybrid workplaces, and new social practices. In S. Armondi & S. Di Vita (Eds.), *Milan. Productions, spatial patterns and urban change* (pp. 73–83). Routledge.
Peck, J. (2014). Entrepreneurial urbanism: Between uncommon sense and dull compulsion. *Series B: Human Geography, 96*(4), 396–401.
Pollio, A. (2020). Making the silicon cape of Africa: Tales, theories and the narration of startup urbanism. *Urban Studies, 57*(13), 2715–2732.
Pradel, M., & Garcia, M. (2021). Policies and Policy Approaches in Cities. In *Companion to urban and regional studies* (pp. 539–561). Wiley-Blackwell.
Rossi, U., & Di Bella, A. (2017). Start-up urbanism: New York, Rio de Janeiro and the global urbanization of technology-based economies. *Environment and Planning A, 49*(5), 999–1018.
Spanò, A. (2017). *I giovani del Sud di fronte alla crisi*. Franco Angeli.
Spanò, A. (2018). *Studiare i giovani nel mondo che cambia*. Franco Angeli.
Swedberg, R. (2000). The social science view of entrepreneurship: Introduction and practical applications. In R. Swedberg (Ed.), *Entrepreneurship: The social science view* (pp. 7–44). Oxford University Press.
Unt, M., Gebel, M., Bertolini, S., Deliyanni-Kouimtzi, V., & Hofäcker, D. (2021). *Social exclusion of youth in Europe: The multifaceted consequences of labour market insecurity*. Policy Press.
Walther, A. (2005). Risks and responsibilities? The individualisation of youth transitions and the ambivalence between participation and activation in Europe. *Social Work and Society, 3*(1), 116–127.
Walther, A. (2006). Regimes of youth transitions. Choice, flexibility and security in young people's experiences across different European contexts. *Young, 14*(2), 119–139.
Woodman, D. (2013). Researching 'ordinary' young people in a changing world: The sociology of generations and the 'missing middle' in youth research. *Sociological Research Online, 18*(1), 179–190.

Index

M. Dodaro, *Unpacking the 'Start-up City'*,
https://doi.org/10.1007/978-3-031-50212-5

SPRINGER NATURE

GPSR Compliance

The European Union's (EU) General Product Safety Regulation (GPSR) is a set of rules that requires consumer products to be safe and our obligations to ensure this.

If you have any concerns about our products, you can contact us on ProductSafety@springernature.com

In case Publisher is established outside the EU, the EU authorized representative is:

Springer Nature Customer Service Center GmbH
Europaplatz 3
69115 Heidelberg, Germany

The manufacturer's authorised representative in the EU is Springer
Nature Customer Service Centre GmbH, Europaplatz 3, 69115 Heidelberg,
Germany. If you have any concerns regarding our products, please
contact ProductSafety@springernature.com

Printed and bound by CPI Group (UK) Ltd, Croydon, CR0 4YY
01/10/2026
02225879-0014